Decanates and Duads

Frances Sakoian
and Louis Acker

Copyright 2009 by Brian R. Wilkin
All rights reserved.

No part of this book may be reproduced or transcribed in any form or by any means, electronic or mechanical, including photocopying or recording or by any information storage and retrieval system without written permission from the author and publisher, except in the case of brief quotations embodied in critical reviews and articles. Requests and inquiries may be mailed to: American Federation of Astrologers, Inc., 6535 S. Rural Road, Tempe, AZ 85283.

ISBN-10: 0-86690-599-5
ISBN-13: 978-0-86690-599-2

Cover Design: Jack Cipolla

Published by:
American Federation of Astrologers, Inc.
6535 S. Rural Road
Tempe, AZ 85283

www.astrologers.com

Printed in the United States of America

Dedicated to

Wilma McIntyre
in appreciation of
her loving help

Contents

Foreword	vii
Introduction	ix
Aries	1
Taurus	11
Gemini	19
Cancer	27
Leo	37
Virgo	47
Libra	57
Scorpio	67
Sagittarius	77
Capricorn	87
Aquarius	97
Pisces	107

Foreword

The technique of using decanates and duads may help to find the reason why the broad characteristics given to each Sun sign do not apply rigidly to all natives. This technique is a refinement that could result in greater accuracy in the work of astrologers and help to establish its validity.

Refinements are necessary in all fields of science or we become stagnant and make the same mistakes over and over again. Progress in any field of endeavor comes from carefully planned changes, and astrology is no exception, despite its antiquity.

In my own profession, which is the forecasting of magnetic storms based upon the heliocentric arrangement of the planets and the angles separating them, I found that my basic discoveries had to undergo constant month to month and year to year refinement before they became sufficiently reliable to be used with confidence and produce forecasts of acceptable accuracy.

I am acquainted with two Leos who are as different as night and day. I also know five Sagittarians who are very much alike and have common interests. Why?

Perhaps the use of decanates and duads would help to explain these variations and even though it would require much more work on the part of the astrologer, it could be well worth the extra effort.

J.H. Nelson

Planetary Rulership, Exaltation and Fall

Planet	Exaltation	Fall	Rulership	Detriment	Accidental Exaltation	Accidental Fall	Accidental Dignity	Accidental Detriment
Sun	Aries	Libra	Leo	Aquarius	1st	7th	5th	11th
Moon	Taurus	Scorpio	Cancer	Capricorn	2nd	8th	4th	10th
Mercury	Aquarius	Leo	Gemini / Virgo	Sagittarius / Pisces	11th	5th	3rd-6th	9th-12th
Venus	Pisces	Virgo	Taurus / Libra	Scorpio / Aries	12th	6th	2nd-7th	8th-1st
Mars	Capricorn	Cancer	Aries	Libra	10th	4th	1st	7th
Jupiter	Cancer	Capricorn	Sagittarius	Gemini	4th	10th	9th	3rd
Saturn	Libra	Aries	Capricorn / Aquarius	Cancer / Leo	7th	1st	10th-11th	4th-5th
Uranus	Scorpio	Taurus	Aquarius / Capricorn	Leo / Cancer	8th	2nd	10th-11th	4th-5th
Neptune	Cancer	Capricorn	Pisces / Sagittarius	Virgo / Gemini	4th	10th	9th-12th	3rd-6th
Pluto	Leo	Aquarius	Scorpio	Taurus	5th	11th	8th	2nd

Introduction

Astrologers have often noticed the differences in personal mannerisms of people who have the same planets prominent in the same signs of their horoscopes. Arguments crediting house position, aspects, and other factors are certainly no unfounded explanation for these differences, but other important items within the horoscope account for many of those differences—items that are neither widely known nor well researched up to this time.

It is not difficult to recognize that in terms of its quality of influence a sign of the zodiac is not an undifferentiated continuum, but that different parts or sections of each sign have slightly and sometimes noticeably different influences.

Several methods are used to determine the different qualities of natives born with planets placed in the same sign. The most widely known and publicized of these is the system of decanates. According to the decanate system, a sign consisting of 30 degrees of arc is subdivided into three segments of 10 degrees each. Each of these segments has been found to have the sub-influence or overtone quality of one of the signs of the triplicity (element) to which the sign in question belongs. The decanate position of planets and angles should be appraised along with the decanates of signs on the house cusps to determine the native's responses to particular people or events.

A planet found in its own decanate or duad, or exalted by decanate or duad, should be interpreted as possessing far greater power than would otherwise be attributed to it. When a planet is double or triple ruler of a duad or decanate and should that planet be found in that duad or decanate, then exceptional abilities pertaining to that planet will be manifested. This can border on genius. Mars, for example, is considered weak or debilitated in Cancer, yet if found in the second or Scorpio decanate of Cancer, it confers the native with courage and resourcefulness in tackling domestic problems and difficulties, thus enabling him or her to maintain personal independence in the face of family opposition.

The first decanate of any sign is the most typically characteristic of the sign in question because the first decanate (the first 10 degrees) of a sign is the sub-ruler of that sign itself.

The second decanate, from 10 to 20 degrees of any sign, has as its sub-ruler the next sign of the Triplicity to which the particular sign in question belongs. This is determined by traveling counterclockwise around the zodiac.

The third decanate, from 20 to 30 degrees of any sign, has as its sub-ruler the third and final sign of the triplicity to which the particular sign in question belongs.

In the following chapters, detailed discussion of the decanates of each sign will make clear the general principles outlined above.

Another important and highly useful method of subdividing the signs is the system of duads. By this approach, each sign is divided into twelve segments of 2½ degrees each, each segment having the sub-influence of one of the twelve signs of the zodiac. The first duad, the first 2½ degrees of each sign, has the same sub-rulership as the sign itself. The second duad, from 2½ to 5 degrees of any sign, has the sub-rulership or overtone influence of the next sign counterclockwise around the zodiac. And so on.

It should be clear that there is much more to astrological interpretation than the mere sign positions of planets or house cusps. *Only* by considering such fine decanate and duad placements of the planets and house cusps, as well as their proximity to fixed stars and the interpretation of their degree placements, can astrologers achieve the high standard of detailed accuracy and the thesis of interpretation that is the hallmark of a high-quality professional.

It is important for students of astrology to learn the use of these factors. It is equally important for experienced horoscope mappers and interpreters to avoid laxity and possible ignorance of these important tools.

Aries

Aries

Sign: Aries   **Ruler:** Mars

Aries Decanate 1: 0-10° Aries   Ruler: Mars

Aries Decanate 1 Duads:

| 0-2½° Aries | 2½-5° Taurus | 5-7½° Gemini | 7½-10° Cancer |
| Ruler: Mars | Ruler: Venus | Ruler: Mercury | Ruler: Moon |

Aries Decanate 2: 10-20° Leo   Ruler: Sun

Aries Decanate 2 Duads:

| 10-12½° Leo | 12½-15° Virgo | 15-17½° Libra | 17½-20° Scorpio |
| Ruler: Sun | Ruler: Mercury | Ruler: Venus | Rulers: Mars, Pluto |

Aries Decanate 3: 20-30° Sagittarius   Ruler: Jupiter

Aries Decanate 3 Duads:

| 20-22½° Sagittarius | 22½-25° Capricorn | 25-27½° Aquarius | 27½-30° Pisces |
| Ruler: Jupiter | Ruler: Saturn | Rulers: Uranus, Saturn | Rulers: Jupiter, Neptune |

Aries

Those with Aries prominent in their horoscopes are active and competitive individuals. They are the great initiators of projects. However, unless there are planets in fixed signs, they lack the steadfastness of purpose to follow through on ventures they initiate. Consequently, as interests and enthusiasms wane, the project suffers.

These natives should learn to think before they act, for impulsive action often results in misdirection and regrets. Even so, undaunted by failure, they are more apt to blaze new trails again.

Self-respect and self-reliance are essential to the psychological well-being of these individuals. They are constantly trying to prove themselves to themselves through action. Efforts to win the approval of others are basically motivated by a desire to garner support that will justify their own self-esteem.

Because Aries is a positive-masculine sign, the natives will have the ability to initiate action toward the realization of their desires and to create meaning in their own lives.

Creative initiative and leadership are qualities inherent to the fire signs. Aries people exhibit these attributes through action and new beginnings. However, natives with Aries prominent are likely to lack the durability and constancy of the sign Leo and the social wisdom intrinsic to the sign Sagittarius. Their success instead depends largely upon their ability to start anew.

Aries individuals are instilled with a basic need for praise and social approval, and when this is forthcoming they enthusiastically tackle the next venture or adventure.

As with all fire signs there is the ever-present danger of self-centeredness and lack of consideration for others. Thus, there is also the need to cultivate an awareness of the rights and needs of others.

Aries Decanates

0-10° Aries
The first decanate of Aries is the Aries-Aries or Mars-Mars decanate. Those with this decanate prominent in the horoscope are apt to be highly competitive and strongly action-oriented. They have been through the Pisces experience and so have a strong inner need to prove themselves through action to themselves and others, and to overcome the muddle and emotional confusion associated with past memories.

These natives are highly competitive, but much of their drive is based on a need to build up their own self-esteem by receiving admiration from others. Obviously this can be either a strength or a weakness. They are apt to be goaded into reckless and foolish actions that go against their better judgments, and need to remember discretion.

Although these natives may be impulsive, impatient, and quick-tempered, they are also blessed with great courage and the ability to make a new start whenever necessary. They initiate things that others only dream about doing.

10-20° Aries
The second decanate of Aries is the Aries-Leo or Mars-Sun decanate. Because of the fixed-sign nature of this decanate, those with it prominent in the horoscope have more staying power and can complete whatever they start. There is organizational ability and the capacity to hold the center of attention that gives these natives a special leadership talent beyond the temporary bravado of the pure Aries influence. This is because of the influence of the Sun, and the fixed-sign nature of Leo.

These natives are robust and strong, with a lot of vitality. They have strong willpower and often a self-centered, authoritative attitude is evident. They are prone to take financial risks, even to gamble. They seek excitement and adventure through competitive sports and in romantic episodes. The Mars-Sun combination gives abundant energy, courage, and self-confidence to these natives. They are capable of magnanimous gestures, but their motives are often colored with egotism and a desire for greater personal prestige.

20-30° Aries

The third decanate of Aries is the Aries-Sagittarius or Mars-Jupiter decanate. This is the decanate of the culturally ambitious. Those with it prominent in the horoscope have the ability to initiate new educational, religious and cultural projects. They have an abundance of enthusiasm for the beliefs and causes they espouse. Because of the mutable quality of Sagittarius and the cardinality of Aries, they can adapt themselves to effective action in a variety of circumstances.

The impulsive Aries nature is tempered with cultural, educational, philosophic and religious insights. They are less self-centered than they might be because they are genuinely interested in including the good of the greater social order into their personal sphere of activity. These expansive actions are often motivated by a desire for greater personal prestige, so these natives must guard against the possibility of showing narrow-minded, self-righteous, fanatical zeal on behalf of their own cultural values and religious beliefs.

These natives like to feel they are an authority in some educational, religious or social field, or that they are the originators of important new concepts in those fields.

Aries Duads

0-2½° Aries

The first duad of Aries is the Aries-Aries or Mars-Pluto duad. Because this duad is part of the Aries-Mars decanate of Aries, the qualities ascribed to the sign Aries and the first decanate of Aries apply to this duad in an intensified manner.

These natives will be energetic, impulsive and action-oriented. Because of the extreme Mars and Pluto influence these natives have a highly developed ability to destroy old conditions and create new ones. They manifest a strong desire to eliminate the outworn conditions of the past and initiate new modes of activity and new fields of expression. The prevailing psychology of these individuals is to let the past die and to take advantage of the present's potential for action and accomplishment.

2½-5° Aries
The second duad of Aries is the Aries-Taurus or Mars-Venus duad. Those with this duad prominent in the horoscope manifest Aries competitiveness and drive where money and the acquisition of material possessions is concerned. Because of the Mars-Venus combination inherent in this duad, the native is apt to be sexually oriented and somewhat sensuous. These natives make good salespeople because the Taurus determination and financial interest is combined with Mars-Aries drive and aggressiveness. Because of the fixed-earth qualities of this duad they are more likely than other Aries natives to complete what they start.

5-7½° Aries
The third duad of Aries is the Aries-Gemini or Mars-Mercury duad. These natives often initiate action, new ideas or scientific and intellectual projects. They have creative vision into the possibilities of the future that can come about through the application of scientific knowledge and technology. They exert leadership by their ability to influence others through innovative ideas and unique solutions to problems or emergency situations.

7½-10° Aries
The fourth duad of Aries is the Aries-Cancer or Mars-Moon duad. These natives tend to be emotionally volatile and excitable. Because of the double cardinal-sign influence of this duad the natives will be even more impulsive than usual, especially in domestic and family affairs. They will defend the family and those with whom they have close emotional relationships. Where finances are concerned there will be a strong protective instinct.

10-12½° Aries
The fifth duad of Aries is the Aries-Leo or Mars-Sun duad. Because this duad is part of the Leo decanate of Aries, the qualities ascribed to the second decanate of Aries apply to this duad in an intensified manner. These natives are apt to express strong leadership qualities and will manifest an unusual talent for organization in managerial affairs. They can have creative talent in the arts, and have a strong desire for personal recognition and fame. They make ardent and enthusiastic lovers.

12½-15° Aries
The sixth duad of Aries is the Aries-Virgo or Mars-Mercury duad. These natives are highly skilled in introducing improved work methods or new procedures involving

health, hygiene, and dress. They are skillful in communication and writing about practical affairs. Because this duad is part of the Leo decanate of Aries, these natives exert leadership and acquire authority through the mastery of practical details in their work. They can acquire high positions in industrial, business, and medical fields.

15-17½° Aries

The seventh duad of Aries is the Aries-Libra or Mars-Venus duad. Aries impulsiveness combined with Leo pride and Libra concern with relationships makes these natives concerned with the impression they make on others even though they like to think of themselves as rugged individualists. They have special talents in promotional and public relations work, and often become involved with the performing arts because of their strong sense of showmanship.

These natives may have unusual artistic talents because of the creative and artistic drive of Leo and the sense of beauty and proportion of Libra. The Sun-Mars-Venus combination means there can be an ardent romantic sense and a strong sex drive.

17½-20° Aries

The eighth duad of Aries is the Aries-Scorpio or Mars-Pluto duad. There is a double influence of Mars and Pluto in this duad, where the initiative of Aries is combined with the emotional intensity and fixity of Scorpio to produce a formidable combination. While there can be great willpower and determination, so that projects will not only be started but finished, inordinate pride and ruthlessness can also be present.

These natives can excel in military careers, engineering, police work, and heavy industry. They are apt to be skilled in starting and leading large-scale corporate business enterprises. They can be relentless fighters for the causes they espouse, and make dangerous enemies. There is a special ability to find creative new uses for old or discarded things. An interest in metaphysics and occult work may be present because of the strong eighth-house Scorpio influence. Because of the double Mars and triple Pluto influence, these natives have a strong, possessive sex drive.

20-22½° Aries

The ninth duad of Aries is the Aries-Sagittarius or Mars-Jupiter duad. Because this duad is part of the Sagittarius decanate of Aries, the qualities ascribed to the third decanate of Aries apply to this duad in an intensified manner.

These natives project much energy and enthusiasm into the causes they espouse, and defend their religion and philosophic beliefs with great vehemence. They are fond of adventure and excitement, especially through sport and travel. They have the ability to initiate and expand enterprises related to philosophy, religion, and higher education, but get themselves into difficulties through impulsiveness or egotistical overconfidence.

22½-25° Aries

The tenth duad of Aries is the Aries-Capricorn or Mars-Saturn duad. The Mars-Saturn combination denotes skill and ability in industrial, business, administrative or military work. These natives can have a broad cultural understanding that enables them to organize or teach these affairs in an effective manner because this duad is part of the Sagittarius decanate of Aries. Their insight into cultural trends gives the ability to structure business and professional affairs in a way that is both effective and profitable.

These natives have a great deal of courage, foresight, and organization, and a capacity for self-discipline and hard work, but they should guard against having a harsh, self-centered attitude.

25-27½° Aries

The eleventh duad of Aries is the Aries-Aquarius or Mars-Uranus-Saturn duad. Those with this duad prominent in the horoscope are extremely independent and resourceful, but will not tolerate interference with their freedom of action. They are receptive to new ideas and have the ability to pioneer new methods of solving problems and getting work done. They have a personal desire for leadership in groups and organizations, and a special ability for organizing new endeavors for clubs or other groups.

Because this duad is part of the Sagittarius decanate, these natives have unusual cultural, humanitarian, and intellectual abilities and insights. Their strong thirst for exciting experiences and unusual adventures often gives them a desire to experiment in various aspects of life. Sometimes they can be predictable because Aquarius is a fixed sign, and at other times they can act in surprising ways. It is hard to know whether they will follow through on a commitment, for example, or abandon it completely. These natives must guard against their unpredictability and the danger of being egotistically perverse.

27½-30° Aries

The twelfth duad of Aries is the Aries-Pisces or Mars-Neptune-Jupiter duad. Those with this duad prominent in the horoscope are apt to initiate actions secretly or behind the scenes. They feel they will avoid opposition by doing things in a quiet and unobtrusive way that may escape the notice of anyone who might interfere with their plans.

Since these natives often act on hunches, their actions frequently seem strange and inexplicable to others. They may get themselves into difficulties by being drawn into secret intrigues of one kind or another. Because their actions are often determined by their imagination they can express themselves in art and have intuitive ability in psychology, religion, and philosophy.

Because of the double Jupiter-Neptune influence they can act in a surprisingly compassionate way for an Aries, particularly if Jupiter or Neptune is found in this duad. (We add Neptune because of historical charts.)

10/Decanates and Dwads

Taurus

Taurus

Sign: Taurus   **Ruler:** Venus

Taurus Decanate 1: 0-10° Taurus   Ruler: Venus

Taurus Decanate 1 Duads:

0-2½° Taurus	2½-5° Gemini	5-7½° Cancer	7½-10° Leo
Ruler: Venus	Ruler: Mercury	Ruler: Moon	Ruler: Sun

Taurus Decanate 2: 10-20° Virgo   Ruler: Mercury

Taurus Decanate 2 Duads:

10-12½° Virgo	12½-15° Libra	15-17½° Scorpio	17½-20° Sagittarius
Ruler: Mercury	Ruler: Venus	Rulers: Mars, Pluto	Ruler: Jupiter

Taurus Decanate 3: 20-30° Capricorn   Ruler: Saturn

Taurus Decanate 3 Duads:

20-22½° Capricorn	22½-25° Aquarius	25-27½° Pisces	27½-30° Aries
Ruler: Saturn	Rulers: Uranus, Saturn	Rulers: Jupiter, Neptune	Ruler: Mars

Taurus

Individuals with the sign Taurus prominent in their horoscopes have the qualities of the earth triplicity and the fixed quadruplicity. They are thus primarily motivated by practical considerations, pursuing goals in a steady, persevering manner. In simple terms, these are goal-oriented individuals who seek to achieve material and emotional security and status.

The Taurus nature as a negative-feminine sign indicates that these natives as a rule do not initiate action or expend energy in offensive conflict. They are more apt to use existing circumstances and situations to obtain maximum material benefit. This, however, does not mean that they lack forcefulness for natives with a strong Taurus chart can be unrelenting and ruthless in conducting defensive battles.

Their sense of values is largely colored by material wealth and status. Thus, they respect or value those who appear opulent and well-dressed. However, they must guard against adopting the view of people as property. Possessiveness and jealousy are often the outcome of such an attitude, with frequent tragic results for these natives, as well as those around them. Should Mars be posited in Taurus, sexual jealousy may lead to violence.

Those with Taurus prominent make loyal and steadfast friends, and they will not abandon those they love. They are generally reliable and trustworthy, and can be counted upon in an emergency.

These individuals will also exhibit a strong love of art, music, beauty, comfort and luxury that confers an appreciation for the finer things in life.

Taurus Decanates

0-10° Taurus
The first decanate of Taurus is the Taurus-Taurus or Venus-Venus decanate. Those with this decanate prominent are strongly oriented toward achieving lasting, permanent results. A relentless determination to satisfy desires for wealth, security and status results from the double fixed-earth influence. The negative side of this can of course be unreasoning, unyielding stubbornness.

The double-Venus, double-Moon (exalted in Taurus) connotations of this decanate endow these natives with a fondness for material comforts and the "good things in life." Artistic and musical talent will be accentuated by their strong, sensuous nature, although this often results in over-indulgence of the physical appetites if carried to excess. Problems in romantic and marital relationships are often the direct result of possessiveness and jealousy on the part of these natives.

Generally, individuals with this decanate prominent in the horoscope are practical, down-to-earth, and averse to wasted effort in non-productive enterprises. They are skillful in money management and make excellent bankers and financiers because they are not inclined to take foolish risks or gambles, and are willing to work slowly and steadily to accomplish their goals.

10-20° Taurus
The second decanate of Taurus is the Taurus-Virgo or Venus-Mercury decanate. These natives, although concerned with money and material values as all Taureans are, will have a detailed, analytical approach toward the realization of their goals of financial and emotional security.

20-30° Taurus
The third decanate of Taurus is the Taurus-Venus or Mars-Capricorn decanate. Mars, exalted in Capricorn, makes these natives ambitious, organized, and cautiously aggressive in their efforts to achieve financial and emotional security. They make good executives and business managers.

Taurus Duads

0-2½° Taurus
The first duad of Taurus is the Taurus-Taurus or Venus-Venus duad. Because this duad is part of the Taurus-Venus decanate of Taurus, the qualities of the sign Taurus and the first decanate of Taurus apply to this duad in an intensified manner.

2½-5° Taurus
The second duad of Taurus is the Taurus-Gemini or Venus-Mercury duad. These natives will be more intellectual, communicative, adaptable, and scientific in their ways of seeking material and emotional security, and less placid and more nervous than the average Taurean. If Mercury is located here the native has mental agility and adaptability that is more pronounced than if Mercury were in any of the other duads of this sign, which normally make one slow in reaching a decision and then obstinate in refusing to change it.

5-7½° Taurus
The third duad of Taurus is the Taurus-Cancer or Venus-Moon duad. Because of the double-Moon influence in this duad (the Moon is exalted in Taurus and rules Cancer), these natives will seek financial security and emotional well-being as a means of providing a safe, secure, and opulent family environment. If the Moon is located here the native will have a much stronger than average orientation toward home and family.

7½-10° Taurus
The fourth duad of Taurus is the Taurus-Leo or Venus-Sun duad. These Taureans are dramatic and creative in expression and use these characteristics to obtain material status and security. The double fixed-sign influence of Taurus and Leo will impart fixed, immovable qualities to any planet in this duad. Their artistic nature is due to the decanate and double-Venus influence. These natives are highly goal-oriented and their fixed determination enables them to carry their creative projects to conclusion. Pluto's exaltation in Leo bestows strong determination and the will to achieve, causing the native to continually seek improvement in the nature and quality of creative projects.

10-12½° Taurus
The fifth duad of Taurus is the Virgo-Virgo or Taurus-Venus-Mercury duad. Because this duad is part of the Virgo decanate of Taurus, the qualities ascribed to the second decanate of Taurus apply to this duad in an intensified manner. Because of this triple

earth-sign influence these natives are intensely practical and down-to-earth in their approach to life, and are apt to enter professions or activities requiring skill and specialized knowledge or training. They are attracted to careers in the fields of medicine, food, or health. Those with this duad prominent in their horoscope seek knowledge and education as a means of achieving greater material security. If Mercury is located here the native possesses even greater practical mental abilities.

12½-15° Taurus
The sixth duad of Taurus is the Taurus- Libra or Venus-Venus duad of Taurus. These natives are cautious, although highly creative and artistic in their personal expressions because of Saturn's exaltation in Libra, combined with Virgo's prudence and the double Venus influence. The exceptional artistic ability supplied by the double-Venus influence of Taurus and Libra may be applied in a practical way, and these individuals can be skillful in business affairs related to the arts or to luxury items. The artistic and musical talent found in this duad is increased if Venus is located here.

15-17½° Taurus
The seventh duad of Taurus is the Taurus-Scorpio or Venus-Mars-Pluto duad. The exaltation of Uranus in Scorpio often makes these natives unpredictable. They sometimes manifest unusual and unexpected behavior, but at other times can be quite fixed and unmovable because of the double fixed-sign nature of Taurus and Scorpio. They can be calculating and clever in achieving their goals, using determination and intuition to produce worthwhile, practical results. In business, scientific, professional, and artistic fields they are creative and resourceful. These natives may be sensuous and highly sexed as a result of the Venus-Mars combination, particularly if the Moon, Sun, Venus or Ascendant is located here. Intense jealously and possessiveness are a danger.

17½-20° Taurus
The eighth duad of Taurus is the Taurus-Sagittarius or Venus-Jupiter duad. These natives are optimistic, confident, and expansive in their efforts to achieve material status and security. The Venus-Jupiter combination confers an interest in religion, art, and music, and the practical business affairs of these natives are often linked to religious and educational institutions especially if Jupiter or Neptune is present. There may be travel of various kinds, foreign or otherwise. These natives seek to consolidate their material status and security by establishing a reputation of solid citizenship within the cultural community. Skillful advertising, intelligent communication, and travel help them achieve prosperity and expand their business efforts.

20-22½° Taurus

The ninth duad of Taurus is the Taurus-Capricorn or Venus-Saturn duad. Because this duad is part of the Capricorn decanate of Taurus, the qualities ascribed to the third decanate of Taurus apply to this duad in an intensified manner. These natives seek material wealth, status, and security through the established institutions and values of business and government. They are very practical and conservative in their approach to life because of the triple-earth signature of this duad, and are exceptionally able in the field of business administration, especially if Saturn is found here. Because of the exaltation of Mars in Capricorn (ruled by Saturn) they are anxious for status in the world in which they move, and often gain recognition as a pillar of society.

22½-25° Taurus

The tenth duad of Taurus is the Taurus-Aquarius or Venus-Uranus duad. Those with this duad prominent use unusual and ingenious intellectual means to achieve material status and emotional security because of the double fixed-sign influence. They have a determination, even stubbornness, in adhering to their own unique system of values. If they ever change their values, it is sudden and unexpected and because of their own self-determinism. They are more unconventional, intellectual, and *avant garde* than the average Taurean. These natives can be successful in businesses that involve advanced technology, electronics, inventions, group and organizational activities, astrology, and occultism. They display intelligence and ingenuity because of Mercury's exaltation in Aquarius. The influence of Capricorn and Saturn causes these natives to be organized and methodical in their practical, creative endeavors. If Uranus is found here there is an unusual ability to apply inspiration and occult knowledge to technologic innovations and practical affairs.

25-27½° Taurus

The eleventh duad of Taurus is the Taurus-Pisces or Venus-Neptune duad. The unusual quality of imagination and inspiration that these natives have gives them artistic and musical creativity, especially if Venus is present. They are drawn to traditional and classical forms of music and art that possess a strong sense of structure and composition because of the Capricorn and double-Venus (Venus rules Taurus and is exalted in Pisces) influence. Their propensity to apply their intuitive faculties to business affairs leads these individuals to have special business and managerial capabilities in the fields of art, luxury items, and the administration of medical, religious, or psychiatric institutions.

27½-30° Taurus

The twelfth duad of Taurus is the Taurus-Aries or Venus-Mars duad. These natives are aggressive in initiating action and excel in sales and promotional work where aggressiveness can be combined with a determination to succeed. Strong qualities of leadership in business affairs will be present if Mars or the Sun is located here. Those with this duad prominent are apt to be concerned with physical beauty and strength, and have a strongly sensuous side to their nature because of the Mars-Venus combination. Since the Sun is exalted in Aries they also have an authoritative manner and a more aggressive bearing than the average easy-going Taurean who only fights defensive battles, and then only when necessary. These natives seek material security through dynamic action.

Gemini

Gemini

Sign: Gemini **Ruler:** Mercury

Gemini Decanate 1: 0-10° Gemini Ruler: Mercury

Gemini Decanate 1 Duads:

0-2½° Gemini	2½-5° Cancer	5-7½° Leo	7½-10° Virgo
Ruler: Mercury	Ruler: Moon	Ruler: Sun	Ruler: Mercury

Gemini Decanate 2: 10-20° Libra Ruler: Venus

Gemini Decanate 2 Duads:

10-12½° Libra	12½-15° Scorpio	15-17½° Sagittarius	17½-20° Capricorn
Ruler: Venus	Rulers: Mars, Pluto	Ruler: Jupiter	Ruler: Saturn

Gemini Decanate 3: 20-30° Aquarius Rulers: Uranus, Saturn

Gemini Decanate 3 Duads:

20-22½° Aquarius	22½-25° Pisces	25-27½° Aries	27½-30° Taurus
Rulers: Uranus, Saturn	Rulers: Jupiter, Neptune	Ruler: Mars	Ruler: Venus

Gemini

Those with Gemini prominent in the horoscope have the qualities of the air triplicity. They are thus intellectually-oriented individuals whose primary concern is ideas and their circulation. Gemini also belongs to the mutable quadruplicity, and therefore these natives have the added characteristic of adaptability. They possess a knack for adjusting to change, whenever and wherever necessary. However this mutable-air temperament may cause the Gemini to be unreliable and fickle in personal and romantic relationships.

The positive-masculine character of Gemini gives these natives the ability to initiate intellectual activity. They take the initiative in communication and literary and scientific work and approach all of these in an intelligent and articulate manner. Their quick wit and sense of humor makes them popular and interesting conversationalists. Much of their work involves the communication of ideas through writing, speech, travel, lecturing or the use of electronic media. If their intelligence and abilities are used to direct their energies in a positive direction, they are purposeful and organized. They can then accomplish a great deal, and recognition and success are often readily attainable.

However these natives tend to be restless and nonconformist. Unlike Taurus, they cannot stand a steady, fixed routine. Life becomes intolerable without newness and change. Thus, they often become confused about their goals, and may lack the necessary steadiness to fully realize their potential. To avoid or at least minimize the effects of such pitfalls they must cultivate the Aquarian-Mercury trait of firmness and constancy of purpose and attention toward the accomplishment of their life objectives.

Gemini Decanates

0-10° Gemini
The first decanate of Gemini is the Gemini-Gemini or Mercury-Mercury decanate. Because of this double-Mercury influence, those with this decanate prominent in the horoscope have unusual intellectual abilities. They possess quick perception and a curious and inquiring intellect that tends to be influenced by whatever impinges on their consciousness. They can, however, be vacillating, indecisive and scattered, with a certain nervous restlessness of mind and body. These natives tend to talk, and are likely to travel about a great deal. They have strong talents in such fields as teaching, writing, administrative work, reporting, advertising, and manual jobs that require dexterity and skill.

10-20° Gemini
The second decanate of Gemini is the Gemini-Libra or Mercury-Venus decanate. These Geminis can have unusual talent in such fields as public relations, diplomacy, psychology, art, and literature. The grace of Venus combined with the intelligence of Mercury can give them charm and the ability to win others over to their point of view. They are willing to impartially examine and consider the ideas of others and, within the limits of their ability, to try to understand both sides of an issue. These natives have a strong need for intellectual companionship and are curious about the thoughts and ideas of others. Their weakness is that they can be swayed and influenced by whomever they are with at the moment, and may gain a reputation for being inconsistent. A certain curiosity about new romantic relationships and what they could offer adds to this reputation.

20-30° Gemini
The third decanate of Gemini is the Gemini-Aquarius or Mercury-Uranus decanate. Those with this decanate prominent in the horoscope often have startling, original, intuitive insights and surprising solutions to problems. They possess a highly organized and intuitive intelligence, especially if Uranus, Saturn or Mercury is found in this decanate. This can manifest as a highly developed scientific ability or an understanding of scientific and metaphysical laws. These natives are open-minded and impartial in the examination of ideas. Their mental outlook is universal and humanitarian. They are strongly influenced by friends and group associates, and often play an active part in clubs and organizations. They tend to set intellectual goals for themselves, and may achieve worthwhile scientific, literary, or humanitarian objectives.

These Geminis can be eccentric and unpredictable at times because they have little tolerance for those who interfere with their intellectual freedom. They demand for themselves the same freedom of inquiry and self-expression they allow others. Because of the Saturn co-rulership of Aquarius, these natives can be surprisingly reserved and serious. They are less likely to engage in verbal frivolities than other Geminis because they reserve their speech until they have something important to say and do not like to engage in small talk.

Gemini Duads

0-2½° Gemini
The first duad of Gemini is the Gemini-Gemini or Mercury-Mercury duad. Because this duad is part of the Gemini-Mercury decanate of Gemini, the qualities ascribed to the sign Gemini and the first decanate of Gemini apply to this duad in an intensified manner. These natives are versatile, adaptable, and skillful in mental pursuits. They make good writers, teachers, lecturers, reporters, news analysts, and scientific investigators. Their primary difficulties are indecisiveness, lack of perseverance, and scattering their resources. They are curious about everything that is going on around them, and want to investigate everything that attracts their attention.

2½-5° Gemini
The second duad of Gemini is the Gemini-Cancer or Mercury-Moon duad. These natives have a strong interest in understanding and communicating about domestic and family affairs, and a curiosity about food, diet, farming, real estate, and business affairs. They are prone to talk about trivial, inconsequential everyday affairs, keeping up an incessant chatter about small things and perhaps annoying others who want to be free to think their own thoughts. Since they have the ability to come up with intelligent solutions to everyday household problems, their practical ingenuity makes them effective in businesses related to food, real estate, farming and home and domestic products and services. They are inclined to be more emotional than the average intellectually detached Gemini.

5-7½° Gemini
The third duad of Gemini is the Gemini-Leo or Mercury-Sun duad. Because of the fixed sign nature of Leo, these natives possess more determination and follow-through than the average Gemini. They have the ability to express their ideas in a dramatic and forceful way that enables them to influence public opinion and take the lead in literary and

scientific fields. There can be a strong intellectual interest in the performing arts, especially as they relate to literary matters. They seek knowledge as a means of achieving authority and leadership in their chosen areas, but can be opinionated and prejudiced in favor of their own point of view. They tend to pursue intellectual pleasures and may show a strong interest in children and their education.

7½-10° Gemini
The fourth duad of Gemini is the Gemini-Virgo or Mercury-Mercury duad. Because of the double-Mercury influence of this duad these natives will have special scientific and intellectual ability. They are more concerned with the practical application of their knowledge than the average Gemini, because Virgo is an earth sign. The mutable sign emphasis indicates adaptability and a tendency to scatter their energies. Those with this duad prominent in the horoscope can draw on past experience and training to solve their problems. They are much more careful and precise concerning detail than the average Gemini, and if Mercury is found in this duad there will be superior reasoning ability and mental capacity.

10-12½° Gemini
The fifth duad of Gemini is the Gemini-Libra or Mercury-Venus duad. Because this duad is part of the Libra decanate of Gemini, the qualities ascribed to the second decanate of Gemini apply to this duad in an intensified manner. These natives have a strong love of art and music, and often exercise unusual talent in these areas. They like and need companionship and can have a strong curiosity about other people and human relationships, which can make them skilled in arbitration and public relations. A strong interest in romantic ties can be spurred by curiosity about the opposite sex. Within the limits of their understanding they seek to exercise justice and fairness in their dealings.

12½-15° Gemini
The sixth duad of Gemini is the Gemini-Scorpio or Mercury-Mars-Pluto duad. Natives with this duad prominent in the horoscope have the ability to uncover secrets and get to the bottom of mysteries. They make good investigators, researchers and writers of detective and mystery stories. This desire to understand hidden causes can give them unusual ability in scientific research or metaphysics. These natives can be blunt and sarcastic in speech. They use a minimum of words to say what they have to say, and are capable of keeping secrets, unlike most Geminis. When they have something to say their words can be as sarcastic and pertinent as a surgeon's knife. Because of the fixed sign nature of Scorpio and Pluto these natives manifest greater follow-through than the aver-

age Gemini. In scholarly as well as practical pursuits they have the ability to initiate new ideas and improve on old ones.

15-17½° Gemini
The seventh duad of Gemini is the Gemini-Sagittarius or Mercury-Jupiter duad. These Geminis have a strong curiosity concerning cultural affairs, religion, philosophy, other countries, and history. Because Gemini and Sagittarius are intellectually oriented, these natives naturally gravitate to institutions of higher learning. They often become scholars, teachers, lecturers, and writers, but may find their knowledge is primarily theoretical, and lacking in practical use. They have a strong love of travel and embark on many long and short journeys. These natives come up with ideas and exploit them to achieve social and intellectual prominence, but because Gemini and Sagittarius are mutable signs, consistency and follow-through may be missing. They often scatter their attention.

17½-20° Gemini
The eighth duad of Gemini is the Gemini-Capricorn or Mercury-Saturn duad. Natives with this duad prominent tend to be purposeful, conservative, and ambitious concerning the use of their ideas and intellectual abilities. They are apt to be eager to achieve status through their ideas, speech, educational writings, and research accomplishments. Their speech is more cautious, guarded, and calculated than the average Gemini, and they possess skill in business and political strategy, especially in advertising and the use of the news media. They tend to worry too much.

20-22½° Gemini
The ninth duad of Gemini is the Gemini-Aquarius or Mercury-Uranus duad. Because this duad is part of the Aquarius decanate of Gemini, the qualities ascribed to the third decanate of Gemini apply to this duad in intensified manner. These natives possess intuitive minds that are original, scientific, and often brilliant, especially if Mercury, Saturn, or Uranus is found here. As a result, they are drawn to scientific, inventive, and metaphysical fields of endeavor. Freedom of inquiry, thought, and communication is as essential to them as the air they breathe. They are friendly, humanitarian, and easy to get along with as long as their intellectual freedom is not threatened. These natives are open-minded and receptive to new ideas and ways of doing things. They have a strong experimental approach to life that opens up new and exciting possibilities for living, but because of their varied interests and unusual approach to life they are regarded as eccentric and unpredictable.

22½-25° Gemini

The tenth duad of Gemini is the Gemini-Pisces or Mercury-Neptune duad. Those with this duad prominent in the horoscope have peculiarly imaginative mental abilities. These can manifest as telepathic awareness or as visionary states in which the native can see things in the mind's eye as if they were actual physical realities. They can use these picture-making abilities in the fields of art, writing, invention, photography, film making and design engineering. They are often in telepathic communication with others who are important to them. Because of the Neptune influence, many of these natives are interested in psychic mysteries and occult literature. There can be an interest in psychology, alternate states of consciousness or sociological matters related to hospitals and institutions. Since Gemini and Pisces are mutable signs, there can be such weaknesses as daydreaming, energy scattering, procrastination, preoccupation with past experiences, confusion, and lack of attention to detail. If these potential weaknesses are overcome, natives can manifest superior intellectual abilities.

25-27½° Gemini

This is the Gemini-Aries or Mercury-Mars duad. These natives tend to be mentally energetic and interested in initiating new ideas. In fact, they can be among the most important intellectual pioneers. Because this duad is part of the Aquarius decanate of Gemini, the intellectual ability of Gemini combines with the intuitive perception of Aquarius and the pioneering drive of Aries; and, because of Pluto's co-rulership of Aries, the ideas these natives come up with are often concerned with new ways of making use of resources that are old, discarded, or ignored. Because of the physical, muscular nature of Mars, these natives will work with their hands and are skilled in the use of tools and machinery. There is a combination of brains and brawn where the hands (ruled by Gemini) are concerned. These natives make good leaders and initiators of group activities.

27½-30° Gemini

The twelfth duad of Gemini is the Gemini-Taurus or Mercury-Venus duad. Those with this duad prominent in the horoscope have a strong intellectual capacity and ideas for business, advertising, and public relations work. They are interested in art, music, and things of beauty and refinement. Because Taurus is a fixed earth sign, they are practical and more likely to finish what they start. They may have a stubborn adherence to their own point of view, although eventually they do carefully weigh all facts. These natives are intellectually geared to making money and often come up with startlingly original ways of doing so because this duad is part of the Aquarius decanate of Gemini. They often have a penetrating insight into economic trends and business affairs.

Cancer

Cancer

Sign: Cancer   **Ruler:** Moon

Cancer Decanate 1: 0-10° Cancer   Ruler: Moon

Cancer Decanate 1 Duads:

0-2½° Cancer	2½-5° Leo	5-7½° Virgo	7½-10° Libra
Ruler: Moon	Ruler: Sun	Ruler: Mercury	Ruler: Venus

Cancer Decanate 2: 10-20° Scorpio   Rulers: Mars, Pluto

Cancer Decanate 2 Duads:

10-12½° Scorpio	12½-15° Sagittarius	15-17½° Capricorn	17½-20° Aquarius
Rulers: Mars, Pluto	Ruler: Jupiter	Ruler: Saturn	Rulers: Uranus, Saturn

Cancer Decanate 3: 20-30° Pisces   Rulers: Jupiter, Neptune

Cancer Decanate 3 Duads:

20-22½° Pisces	22½-25° Aries	25-27½° Taurus	27½-30° Gemini
Rulers: Jupiter, Neptune	Rulers: Mars, Pluto	Ruler: Venus	Ruler: Mercury

Cancer

Cancer is of the water triplicity and the cardinal quadruplicity. Thus, natives with this sign prominent in the horoscope are basically concerned with emotional issues and are continually engaged in activity in response to environmental needs. In the case of Cancer, this action is usually a reaction, for this sign is a negative-feminine sign which does not initiate action on its own internally-motivated impulses in the manner that Aries would. Cancer is the sign of motherhood, and just as the actions of a mother are dictated by the needs of her child, so are the actions of an individual with Cancer prominent dictated by the needs of the family or those in the immediate household or environment.

It should not be forgotten that Jupiter and Neptune are exalted in Cancer, conferring these individuals with a desire for inner peace and harmony and often causing them to seek out religious or spiritual precepts and guidance that can be incorporated into daily life.

Often, these natives are highly sensitive to the point of being psychic in their awareness of the feelings, thoughts, and motivations of those around them, and it is here that difficulties are apt to arise. Such extreme sensitivity to external stimuli can cause the moods and feelings of these individuals to fluctuate constantly in response to the influence of environmental factors.

Indeed it is conceivable that such outside emotional pressures could cause emotional confusion and frustration. However, in the case of those with Cancer prominent, should the outside world become too frightening, their Moon-Jupiter nature will incline them to withdraw into a private domain as an escape from that which is a threat to their well-being. In that event there is erected a psychological barrier while waiting for a safer time to renew activity. The most serious difficulty encountered under such conditions would be the individual's ability, in his or her psychological withdrawal, to determine the appropriate point at which he or she should rejoin the mainstream of humanity and resume activity. This requires fixity of purpose (Moon exalted in Taurus) and a great degree of objectivity—characteristics that should be cultivated and properly developed by these individuals.

Cancer Decanates

0-10° Cancer

The first decanate of Cancer is the Cancer-Cancer or Moon-Moon decanate. It has a double-Moon influence, indicating natives who are emotional and sensitive, and more concerned with family and domestic affairs than other Cancers. Their moods are unpredictable because their emotions undergo many changes and fluctuations; at times they are calm, content, and serene, and at other times discontented, distraught, and upset. They tend to take on the coloring and moods of those in their immediate surroundings, which makes their environment a deciding factor in the state of their well-being or lack of it. They are apt to become attached to possessions that have sentimental value. Generally there is a strong interest in cooking and food. These natives can be prone to feel overly emotional at slights, even when none is intended.

10-20° Cancer

The second decanate of Cancer is the Cancer-Scorpio or Moon-Mars-Pluto decanate. Because Scorpio is a fixed sign, these natives have more willpower and determination than the average Cancer. Although Cancer and Scorpio are feminine signs and wait for things to come to them, the Mars and Pluto rulership of this decanate gives the ability to fight a defensive battle that is relentless and unyielding. Once they have set out to accomplish a task they do so with power and thoroughness. If Mars is found in this decanate it is not as weak and debilitated as it would be in another decanate of Cancer.

These natives can be intensely emotional about sexual and romantic relationships, so jealousy and possessiveness can become a problem. They have considerable ability in do-it-yourself projects because this decanate depicts action in the home and resourcefulness in solving domestic problems; but there are often conflicts with the mother or with other parental figures. There can be a strong interest in mystical and occult pursuits because Uranus is exalted in Scorpio and Pluto rules that sign. These natives often have unusual psychic abilities.

20-30° Cancer
The third decanate of Cancer is the Cancer-Pisces or Moon-Neptune-Jupiter decanate. These natives have a strong inclination to incorporate religious and spiritual values into their home and family life, seeking to cultivate a peaceful, spiritual atmosphere in their domestic environment. Their home is often used as a place of healing and refuge.

These natives have highly developed psychic ability. For example, Madame Blavatsky had this decanate on her Ascendant. They have active imaginations and artistic talent because Jupiter and Neptune are exalted in Cancer and co-rule Pisces. They are kind and sympathetic, with a great understanding for the emotional, physical, and spiritual needs of others. Unfortunately, there can be a tendency toward inertia, and a tendency to ignore the need for cleanliness and order in the environment.

Cancer Duads

0-2½° Cancer
The first duad of Cancer is the Cancer-Cancer or Moon-Moon duad. Because this duad is part of the Cancer-Moon decanate of Cancer, the qualities ascribed to the sign Cancer and the first decanate of Cancer apply to this duad in an intensified manner. Those with this duad prominent in the horoscope are strongly oriented toward home and family, especially if the Moon is located here. They excel as homemakers. Women with this duad prominent are extremely feminine, and make excellent mothers and good cooks. If there are adverse aspects involving this duad they could have an unfortunate tendency to spoil their children. These natives are highly imaginative and often intuitive regarding the moods and feelings of others, but should guard against excessive emotional excitability and moodiness. Their emotional ups and downs can exasperate others, making relationships difficult. This duad can indicate business abilities in food handling and processing, farming, restaurants, real estate, and home and domestic products and services.

2½-5° Cancer
The second duad of Cancer is the Cancer-Leo or Moon-Sun duad. These natives can be good actors in playing emotional roles on and off stage because they have a tendency toward emotional self-dramatization. Even when they act like typical

shy Cancers their shyness is designed in such a way as to gain personal attention and recognition. The forceful, creative expression of Leo, combined with the double-Cancer emphasis of this duad, can make these natives surprisingly energetic, active, and self-assertive. They can express their creative urges through gourmet cooking and lavish entertaining in the home, which they often turn into a showplace. Women with this duad prominent are highly maternal and dote on their children. Parents with this duad prominent can be so proud of their children to be blind to their obvious faults.

5-7½° Cancer
The third duad of Cancer is the Cancer-Virgo or Moon-Mercury duad. Those with this duad prominent in the horoscope make superb cooks, often combining the health food consciousness of Virgo with Cancer's ability to make food tasty to the palate. The average Cancer tends to be emotional and sentimental, but these natives are mentally alert and more logical than most. The Virgo concern with hygiene, neatness, and cleanliness, combined with Cancer's concern for home, make them orderly and clean housekeepers. They will go to great lengths to protect their family's health through good hygiene, proper diet, adequate clothing, and medical care. There is the ability to organize the family budget and tend to business affairs, especially those related to restaurants and home and domestic products and services, and all businesses related to food, clothing, and health. Because this duad is part of the Cancer decanate the double-cardinal sign influence combines with the Virgo capacity for efficiency and methodology to provide an ability for effective, decisive action in family and business affairs.

7½-10° Cancer
The fourth duad of Cancer is the Cancer-Libra or Moon-Venus duad. These natives have highly developed emotional sensitivity in social situations. Harmonious relationships and beauty in the home are essential for their happiness. Because of their emotional sensitivity their feelings can be easily hurt, but they can be kind and sympathetic to others because of intuitive rapport with the moods and feelings of those around them. Since there is a triple-cardinal emphasis arising from the sign Cancer, the Cancer decanate, and the Libra duad, these native will be extremely active socially and domestically. The are likely to carry on social activities in their home, and are motivated toward marriage as a means of establishing a secure home life. These natives can be skilled in public relations and have an understanding of mass psychology. Women with this duad prominent can have unusual femininity, grace, charm, and sensitivity. Men with this duad prominent often have an ability to emotionally understand and appreciate women.

10-12½° Cancer

The fifth duad of Cancer is the Cancer-Scorpio or Moon-Mars-Pluto duad. Because this duad is part of the Scorpio decanate of Cancer, the qualities ascribed to the second decanate of Cancer apply to this duad in an intensified manner. Since Cancer and Scorpio are both water signs, these natives will manifest great emotional intensity in their self-expression. The double-Scorpio influence associated with this duad gives these individuals greater follow-through and thoroughness than the average Cancer. If Mars, Uranus, or Pluto is found in this duad the native may be intensely determined in actions, show strong willpower, and in some cases may have an understanding of occult mysteries. There can also be the ability to initiate new and better ways of doing work in industrial, scientific, occult, and business fields. These natives, if pushed too far, can be prone to violent emotional outbursts. There can be considerable skill in corporate business affairs, which is certainly true of the United States. These individuals can be highly emotional concerning the use of joint finances, and when dealing in cooperative financial enterprises or things pertaining to family finances.

It is interesting to note that the Sun in the United States horoscope is found in this duad, indicating that the American people are capable of more toughness, energy, and determination than would otherwise be indicated by the sensitive sign of Cancer. We are a nation born in resolution, as indicated by Uranus exalted in Scorpio. Because of the regenerative factor of Scorpio and the maternal qualities of Cancer, we have attempted to mother the world just as those with this duad prominent know how to help those who come to them with problems. However, after receiving assistance, its recipients are required to help themselves.

12½-15° Cancer

The sixth duad of Cancer is the Cancer-Sagittarius or Moon-Jupiter duad. Because of the double-Jupiter emphasis arising from Jupiter ruling Sagittarius and exalted in Cancer, these natives have a strong interest in bringing religious and cultural values into the home and family life. The Scorpio influence of the decanate in which this duad falls means they will regard higher education and family participation in cultural and religious activities as an avenue of personal and family improvement. These natives are fond of travel and living in faraway places. They could bring visitors from foreign countries or faraway places into the home. They seek to help those less fortunate than themselves by visiting hospitals and working with cultural institutions. They are generous and expansive in the expression of their feelings.

15-17½° Cancer

The seventh duad of Cancer is the Cancer-Capricorn or Moon-Saturn duad. Those with this duad prominent in the horoscope are conservative, reserved, and ambitious. They are reluctant to openly express their inner feelings because doing so could lead to emotional frustration. Even though they may appear shy and retiring they can be shrewd business people, concerned with financial security for their family and their own retirement. Their strong business sense is indicated by a number of factors. Capricorn is a business-oriented sign; this duad is part of the Scorpio decanate, which is concerned with corporate business or using other people's money; and the Moon rules Cancer and is concerned with finances through its exaltation in Taurus. As a result, these natives often amass large fortunes or holdings of land and property, and always have a nest egg tucked away for future family needs.

Because Cancer and Capricorn are both cardinal signs, these individuals are busy with their work and capable of decisive action whenever necessary. Women with this duad prominent seek marriage with older or more established business people or executives who can give them status and financial security, thus reinforcing a natural tendency in Cancer women who have Capricorn on the seventh house in their solar chart. Parents with this duad prominent discipline their children more than most Cancer parents usually do. There is also a double-Mars influence (Mars rules Scorpio and is exalted in Capricorn) that endows these natives with energy and initiative, and produces individuals stronger than the average Cancer, especially if Mars is located here.

17½-20° Cancer

The eighth duad of Cancer is the Cancer-Aquarius or Moon-Uranus-Saturn duad. These natives manifest sudden and unpredictable emotional behavior, and can have frequent and sudden changes of residence. They have intuition and occult abilities because of the double-Uranus influence (Uranus is exalted in Scorpio and rules Aquarius). If Uranus, Neptune, or Pluto is found in this duad, these abilities will be strongly marked. Those with this duad prominent in the horoscope often use the home as a meeting place for friends and group activities; close friends can become like members of the family. The home may be equipped with motions, electronic gadgets or unusual furniture, decor or architecture. Unlike most Cancers, these natives demand freedom in their family relationships so as to be able to pursue their own interests and come and go as they please. They will experiment in applying the latest theories of child psychology to their children, and will be strongly interested in their intellectual development. They want their children to develop in a free and unique way.

20° to 22 ½° Cancer

The ninth duad of Cancer is the Cancer-Pisces or Moon-Neptune-Jupiter duad. Because this duad is part of the Pisces decanate of Cancer, the qualities ascribed to the third decanate of Cancer apply to this duad in an intensified manner. Those with this decanate prominent in the horoscope can manifest strong psychic and imaginative abilities, especially if Neptune or Jupiter is present. This is due to the triple Neptune-Jupiter influence that arises out of the exaltation of these planets in Cancer and their rulership of Pisces. These natives are highly emotional about their religious, spiritual, educational, and cultural beliefs, and often tend toward mystical practices, meditation, or religious devotion in some form; this results from the triple water sign influence. They must guard against involvement in astral plane psychism, fanatical devotion to a guru or cult, and undesirable, subliminal psychic influences and suggestions; this is because they are susceptible to subconscious telepathic influences. There is also danger they will become immersed in past memories and misfortunes and neglect present responsibilities. The imagination often leads to artistic and musical abilities.

22½-25° Cancer

The tenth duad of Cancer is the Cancer-Aries or Moon-Mars duad. Natives with this duad prominent in the horoscope are prone to impulsive emotional reactions, especially in response to things that trigger emotional memories, because this duad is part of the Pisces decanate and is concerned with the unconscious mind. They can use their intuition and the double cardinal sign emphasis of this duad by taking decisive action and overcoming the inertia of past conditioning. Their active subconscious may make them emotionally volatile in their behavior. If Mars or Pluto is found here the native can show initiative and resourcefulness in business, especially businesses related to food, domestic products and services, or matters of cultural interest. They try to put their religious views into action.

25-27½° Cancer

The eleventh duad of Cancer is the Cancer-Taurus or Moon-Venus duad. Those with this duad prominent in the horoscope are fond of comfort and elegance in the home. If it is not a place of beauty and harmony, it is not a home for them. They can be talented artists, interior decorators, musicians, and actors because the combined artistic qualities of Taurus and Pisces give a double-Venus influence. Because of the fixed-sign nature of Taurus and the tenacity of Cancer, these natives do not give up easily in seeking their goals They are willing to adapt their methods to the requirements of the situation because of the mutability and adaptability of the Pisces decanate, but their desire for domestic comfort and security remains constant. These Cancers have a strong business sense, especially in matters related to home, food, domestic products and service, and art or luxury items. They have charming and gracious personal mannerisms and an intuitive, sympathetic understanding of those around them, especially family members. Women with this duad prominent often have unusual beauty and charm and portray the very essence of femininity.

27½-30° Cancer
The twelfth duad of Cancer is the Cancer-Gemini or Moon-Mercury duad. These natives display more intellectual tendencies than the average emotional Cancer, and are curious about the psychological, emotional, or psychic aspects of life. Their reason can be distorted by subconscious emotional factors, but Mercury's influence can help them achieve insights into the workings of their own subconscious. They can be skilled in such fields as psychology, creative writing, and the education of small children. Because this duad is part of the Pisces decanate, there is a double mutable sign emphasis that could appear either as vacillation or as adaptability in action. Natives with this duad prominent are prone to much travel and many changes of residence.

Leo

Leo

Sign: Leo   **Ruler:** Sun

Leo Decanate 1: 0-10° Leo   Ruler: Sun

Leo Decanate 1 Duads:

0-2½° Leo	2½-5° Virgo	5-7½° Libra	7½-10° Scorpio
Ruler: Sun	Ruler: Mercury	Ruler: Venus	Rulers: Mars, Pluto

Leo Decanate 2: 10-20° Sagittarius   Ruler: Jupiter

Leo Decanate 2 Duads:

10-12½° Sagittarius	12½-15° Capricorn	15-17½° Aquarius	17½-20° Pisces
Ruler: Jupiter	Ruler: Saturn	Rulers: Uranus, Saturn	Rulers: Jupiter, Neptune

Leo Decanate 3: 20-30° Aries   Rulers: Mars, Pluto

Leo Decanate 3 Duads:

20-22½° Aries	22½-25° Taurus	25-27½° Gemini	27½-30° Cancer
Ruler: Mars	Ruler: Venus	Ruler: Mercury	Ruler: Moon

Leo

Those with Leo prominent in the horoscope are by virtue of Leo's membership in the fire triplicity endowed with an energetic, enthusiastic, positive disposition, and thus they exhibit a character imbued with the qualities of strong willpower and leadership. Likewise, Leo's nature as a positive-masculine sign of the fixed quadruplicity endows these individuals with great determination, durability, and the initiative and forbearance to inaugurate activity without awaiting opportune circumstances. Thus it is that natives of a strong Leo bent possess an immense, and seemingly inexhaustible supply of energy and willpower that is the key to their charisma and leadership ability. While Aries possesses the ability or drive to initiate action, Leo is endowed with a managerial capacity enabling those of its sign to achieve and maintain themselves as the central figures in endeavors extending over long periods of time.

Self-consciousness and pride, both characteristics of Leo, incline these individuals to view themselves as actors upon the stage of life, needing to impress their audience. Thus, those with Leo prominent are fond of contests requiring individual skill and prowess, often provided by games and sports. They thrive upon the excitement generated by competition, and the opportunity to prove themselves to others.

This need to impress others, should it be carried to extremes or expressed unwisely, can often become the source of their own undoing. Over-extension of personal resources and unwitting failures due to a lack of practicality and realism will convince even Leos that there are limitations to the scope of their power. This they must learn to recognize early, and thus avoid embarrassment and disgrace. If not, they are more than likely to experience losses through gambling, financial speculation or romantic conquests of an ill-advised nature. The proper exercise of wisdom will always open new avenues for creativity and self-expression in the lives of these natives.

Leo Decanates

0-2½° Leo
The first decanate of Leo is the Leo-Leo or Sun-Sun decanate. Those with this decanate prominent are endowed with tremendous vitality and personal authority. They can have unusual physical strength and willpower even if they become ill or fatigued—especially if the Sun, Mars, or Pluto is found here. They have tremendous recuperative powers.

Because of the double fixed-fire emphasis there is tremendous staying power, determination, and self-confidence, giving these natives a capacity for leadership and a strong charisma. The negative expression of this decanate is a stubborn ego-centeredness, pride, and the need to be the center of attention. They are prone to identify themselves with their own egocentric point of view, and may lack objectivity and humility.

In highly developed natives there can be a strong sense of spiritual power and the advanced use of the will through concentrated attention. Because they possess powers of creation that enable them to give form and life to their ideas, many fine artisans, actors, sculptors, inventors, and craftsmen have this decanate prominent.

10-20° Leo
The second decanate of Leo is the Leo-Sagittarius or Sun-Jupiter decanate. Those with this decanate prominent in the horoscope are concerned with cultural leadership. The influence of Sagittarius and its co-rulers Jupiter and Neptune gives these natives an innate understanding of prevailing social and cultural trends in politics, education, religion, philosophy, and law. They influence others and gain power and leadership through their ability to mold public opinion.

Often it is as if these individuals are alone in a crowd. They can maintain a strong sense of their own direction even against a tide of popular opinion; however, their understanding of mass psychology can give them an air of aloofness. Because of the expansive nature of Jupiter these natives attempt large and impressive enterprises and endeavors. They may seek to impress others by entertaining in an opulent and magnificent way. If these tendencies are carried too far they can overreach themselves, incurring debts and obligations that are difficult or impossible to fulfill.

These Leos are fond of travel and they desire superiority in sport. There can also be a desire to make an important cultural contribution that leaves a personal mark in history, even if only in a small way.

20-30° Leo
The third decanate of Leo is the Leo-Aries or Sun-Mars-Pluto decanate. Those with this decanate prominent in the horoscope have a lot of initiative and the energy to start new projects even though the fixed sign quality of Leo often makes its natives indifferent to new possibilities. The fixity of Leo gives the ability to see projects through to the end. These Leo are self-sufficient and willing to provide for their own needs. They are highly competitive and want to be first in whatever is important to them, but must guard against an egotistical need to be the central authority figure and a self-centeredness that can interfere with their happiness.

Because Pluto is exalted in Leo and co-rules Aries, it has a double influence in this decanate. It gives the ability to reuse discarded materials that others would consider junk. Inherent in this ability is the means of regenerating personal habits and overcoming weaknesses, providing the native will set ego aside and admit that a problem exists.

These natives often have a strong, muscular build with physical strength or prowess as well as personal magnetism and vitality; but excessive drinking caused by an unquenchable thirst can be their undoing despite their tremendous capacity for holding liquor. Because of their high degree of masculinity, men with this decanate prominent have great appeal to women. Women with this decanate prominent can be authoritative and self-assertive to the point of competing with men in some manner.

Leo Duads

0-2½° Leo
The first duad of Leo is the Leo-Leo or Sun-Sun duad. Because this duad is part of the Leo-Sun decanate of Leo, the qualities ascribed to the sign Leo and the first decanate of Leo apply to this duad in an intensified manner. These natives are self-confident and can tackle large or difficult projects. They are able to overcome difficult obstacles because of their optimism and creative powers. Once a goal is chosen they are not easily deterred

by opposition, difficulty, or frustration. The power of highly-developed natives of this duad comes from their ability to focus their attention and energy into useful work in a sustained and single-minded way. These Leos are magnanimous, creative, and authoritative, preferring to pursue both work and play with complete dedication to the moment; but pride, egotism, or stubbornness can be their downfall. If the Sun or Pluto is found here there will be added vitality, magnetism, and power.

2½-5° Leo
The second duad of Leo is the Leo-Virgo or Sun-Mercury duad. These natives have a cautious and practical approach to the pursuit of their creative endeavors. They are conscious of detail and work more methodically than the average Leo, who is only concerned with large-scale issues. While other Leos rely on others to do practical, menial, or detailed tasks, Leos of this duad are willing to serve as well as lead. The mental nature of Mercury makes them good teachers for young people, and they are concerned about the health and hygiene of those in their charge. These individuals impress others through their interest in clothing and their attention to personal appearance which leads them to maintain their health through exercise and proper diet. Because of the mutable quality of Virgo, these Leos are willing to adapt to changing circumstances when it is necessary and practical to do so.

5-7½° Leo
The third duad of Leo is the Leo-Libra or Sun-Venus duad. Because Leo and Libra are both artistic signs, these natives can excel in all forms of artistic creativity. They are highly romantic and ardent in love relationships, and are attractive to the opposite sex because of their unusual charm, grace, and magnetism. The self-confidence of Leo and Libra's desire for relationships gives them special ability in public relations, performing arts, and diplomatic tasks. They also make effective sales people because the Leo fixity contributes perseverance. Parents with this duad prominent will be kind but firmly just in the handling of children.

7½-10° Leo
The fourth duad of Leo is the Leo-Scorpio or Sun-Pluto-Mars duad. Inherent in this duad is a triple-Pluto influence because Pluto is exalted in the Leo sign and decanate and rules Scorpio. Since Leo and Scorpio are both fixed signs, indicating saying power and determination, it becomes obvious why this is one of the most powerful duads of the zodiac. These natives have tremendous resourcefulness, powers of regeneration, and intense willpower and determination. They can be relentless in achieving their goals and

demonstrate a remarkable ability to improve existing conditions because of their initiative, vitality, energy, and self-confidence. They often have the piercing, penetrating eyes—X-ray eyes—associated with certain Pluto, Scorpio, and Leo types. If Pluto or Mars is located here these already strong attributes are intensified.

10-12½° Leo

The fifth duad of Leo is the Leo-Sagittarius or Sun-Jupiter duad. Because this duad is part of the Sagittarius decanate of Leo, the qualities ascribed to the second decanate of Leo apply to this duad in an intensified manner. Those with this duad prominent in the horoscope are philosophically and culturally-oriented leaders, especially in educational, cultural, and religious fields. They are fond of sports, outdoor activities, and travel. These natives often are attracted to politics and law because they possess a strong sense of justice and fair play. They avoid doing anything that would tarnish their reputation and are generous and magnanimous to others, but can suffer from a foolish over-optimism that causes them to assume more obligations than they can handle. These Leos inspire confidence in others because of their own enthusiasm and self-confidence.

12½-15° Leo

The sixth duad of Leo is the Leo-Capricorn or Sun-Saturn duad. Those with this duad prominent in the horoscope make effective leaders and administrators because of the organizational abilities of both Saturn and Capricorn, the charisma of Leo, and the foresight of Sagittarius (indicated by the Jupiter decanate to which this duad belongs). These natives are more reserved and less flamboyant in personal behavior than the average Leo, maintaining an air of reserved personal dignity that causes them to be considered demanding taskmasters. This duad indicates disciplinarians who expect a high degree of achievement from their children. Many of these individuals are attracted to politics or corporate administration. Because of the cardinal sign nature of Capricorn and the exaltation of Mars in Capricorn, they are capable of decisive action at the strategic time.

15-17½° Leo

The seventh duad of Leo is the Leo-Aquarius or Sun-Saturn-Uranus duad. Those with this duad prominent are more impersonal and reserved than the average Leo since the mind rules here, as well as the heart. They have many friends and group associates and often assume a leadership role in group or organizational affairs. They do not submit easily to external authority, and resent any intrusion on their self-determination more than most Leos do.

These natives have unusual ideas and inventive minds as well as the necessary energy and willpower to express their ideas. They can excel in such fields as science, technology, and engineering, and are apt to speculate in new industrial technologies. At times these Leos may appear contrary and contradictory to those around them because they are subject to sudden and explainable shifts of viewpoint and attitude. But at the same time the double fixed-sign emphasis of this duad can give them a tendency toward stubbornness and perversity. They are prone to unusual situations and sudden changes in their romantic life.

17½-20° Leo

The eighth duad of Leo is the Leo-Pisces or Sun-Jupiter-Neptune duad. There is a double Jupiter-Neptune influence because these planets rule Pisces and the Sagittarius decanate to which this duad belongs. As a result, there is a strong creative imagination and artistic bent that can combine with Leo's self-expressiveness to produce talented artists, musicians, and actors. These natives are generous and kind toward others, especially these less fortunate. They often assume leadership roles in educational, religious, and charitable institutions, which gives them a sense of importance and self-fulfillment. They are highly romantic and idealistic concerning love and romance, and their fortunes in love have a strong impact on their general mood and disposition. These Leos like to surround themselves with an air of drama, romance, and mystery. They can have intuitive and prophetic abilities, or prophetic dreams.

20-22½° Leo

The ninth duad of Leo is the Leo-Aries or Sun-Mars-Pluto duad. Because this duad is part of the Aries decanate of Leo, the qualities ascribed to the third decanate of Leo apply to this duad in an intensified manner. Those with this duad prominent have abundant energy and great resourcefulness and self-reliance. The cardinal Aries and fixed Leo combination makes possible the initiative to start projects, and the determination to finish them. These natives are adept at improving present methodologies and recycling discarded resources because of the triple Pluto influence inherent in this duad.

These natives have powers of intense concentration or focused attention that give them considerable creative and spiritual power. Their courage and self-confidence enable them to tackle problems that would deter others. They are competitive and proud. They wish to be recognized as authorities and to excel in the areas important to them, and are never completely satisfied unless they are first and best.

22½-25° Leo

The tenth duad of Leo is the Leo-Taurus or Sun-Venus duad. These natives are artistic and creative because Taurus and Leo are both artistic signs. These Leos are often attracted to art, music, entertainment, and the theater. They are usually highly sexed and can be very sensuous because of the romantic nature of Leo and the sensuality of Taurus and Venus. The sex drive is intensified by the desire principle of Mars acting through the Aries decanate to which this duad belongs. These natives can be jealous and possessive in romance or marriage. They can have a strong business sense and are prone to financial speculation because of Leo's concern with speculation and Taurus' concern with money and property. The Aries decanate influence can make them competitive in their field.

25-27½° Leo

The eleventh duad of Leo is the Leo-Gemini or Sun-Mercury duad. Those with this duad prominent in the horoscope are creative in such fields as writing and technological innovation. With their quick wit and sense of humor they often make good playwrights, comedians, and entertainers. They are often skilled in working with children and their education. Although inclined to plan their actions before embarking on any new endeavor, impulsiveness of speech can be a source of difficulty for these natives. They are fond of debates and games of mental skill, and wish to be recognized as an authority in some intellectual field. Because of the active nature of Aries and Gemini these natives get around from place to place more than the average fixed Leo.

27½-30° Leo

The twelfth duad of Leo is the Leo-Cancer or Sun-Moon duad. These natives take pride in family, often boasting about their children and spending much time with them. They are more sensitive than the average Leo and their feelings can be hurt, although they are too proud to show it. They are often more impulsive than other Leos because of Moon influences arising from their subconscious, combined with the double cardinal emphasis of Cancer and the Aries decanate in which this duad falls. Their emotional intensity and sensitivity can make these natives skilled actors and dramatists. They can have business dealings or financial speculation involving restaurants, farming, real estate, and food processing and distribution. They have a strong need for financial security for themselves and their family.

Virgo

Virgo

Sign: Virgo   **Ruler:** Mercury

Virgo Decanate 1: 0-10° Virgo   Ruler: Mercury

Virgo Decanate 1 Duads:

0-2½° Virgo	2½-5° Libra	5-7½° Scorpio	7½-10° Sagittarius
Ruler: Mercury	Ruler: Venus	Rulers: Mars, Pluto	Ruler: Jupiter

Virgo Decanate 2: 10-20° Capricorn   Ruler: Saturn

Virgo Decanate 2 Duads:

10-12½° Capricorn	12½-15° Aquarius	15-17½° Pisces	17½-20° Aries
Ruler: Saturn	Rulers: Uranus, Saturn	Ruler: Jupiter, Neptune	Ruler: Mars

Virgo Decanate 3: 20-30° Taurus   Ruler: Venus

Virgo Decanate 3 Duads:

20-22½° Taurus	22½-25° Gemini	25-27½° Cancer	27½-30° Leo
Ruler: Venus	Ruler: Mercury	Ruler: Moon	Ruler: Sun

Virgo

The sign Virgo is of the earth triplicity and like those with Taurus prominent, individuals of Virgo temperament are primarily motivated by practical considerations. Because Virgo is one of the mutable quadruplicity, these practical objectives are achieved or realized through adaptation to changing circumstances that are based upon past experiences rather than by virtue of the fixed determination characteristic of Taurus.

Mercury's rulership of Virgo confers upon these natives a high degree of intelligence, but unlike Gemini, also ruled by Mercury, their mental ability is of an applied, practical nature rather than the intellectual, theoretical nature of Gemini. These individuals acquire knowledge through practical work experience and when they are formally trained, it is to acquire a definite skill or professional expertise in a chosen field of endeavor.

Because Virgo is a negative-feminine sign, it imparts to those of its bent the practical skills necessary to improve and make proper use of existing conditions. Those with this sign prominent feel lost without a meaningful job that confers status and purpose to their lives. Thus, their acquisition of specialized, practical knowledge often ensures job security and reasonable financial rewards. This is particularly true of those Virgos engaged in the medical field.

The concern of these natives for practical work and service leads to their constant involvement in matters of detail. But this concern for detail, should it be carried to excess, can induce a distorted view of reality, for natives of the Virgo disposition often tend to overlook the main issues of life while attempting to achieve perfection in their particular area of expertise. Constant attention to practical duty often leads to loneliness and social isolation.

Those of Virgo temperament, like natives of other earth signs, enjoy the material comforts of life, although they are likely to alternate between frugality and extravagance in their acquisition of these pleasures.

Virgo Decanates

0-10° Virgo

The first decanate of Virgo is the Virgo-Virgo or Mercury-Mercury decanate. Those with this decanate prominent in the horoscope strongly manifest typical Virgo characteristics. They are concerned with health, cleanliness, hygiene, proper diet, and work, and usually handle practical responsibilities efficiently, both in the home and on the job.

They often are attracted to careers as doctors or nurses, or jobs related to medicine, health and hygiene, or to work related to food preparation and distribution. Since they are particular about dress and personal appearance, and have a sense of style where clothing and dress are concerned, dress design and the clothing industry are also possible sources of employment.

These natives enjoy intellectual conversations with friends, relatives, and coworkers, but they are shy when dealing with strangers or with emotional issues. They have a good memory for detail, and can handle figures or work that requires precision and manual dexterity. Their keen powers of observation often allow them to notice things going on around them that others miss. If Mercury is found in this decanate the native's mental skill will be of superior quality.

10-20° Virgo

The second decanate of Virgo is the Virgo-Capricorn or Mercury-Saturn decanate. These natives make skillful administrators and have a high degree of organizational ability. They are hard working and anxious for success in their chosen field with a highly-developed capacity for mental organization and concentration that makes them good draftsmen, engineers, mathematicians, scientists, skilled craftsmen, and researchers. To others they seem to have endless patience in handling details and performing exactly precise tasks, especially if Saturn is found in this decanate.

In personal mannerism they are reserved, taciturn, and dignified, leaning toward traditional social, moral, and ethical values. These Virgos are not interested in ideas per se, only in their practical applications.

20-30° Virgo

The third decanate of Virgo is the Virgo-Taurus or Mercury-Venus decanate. These natives are outgoing and more concerned with creature comforts than the average Virgo. The have a strong business sense that makes them good clothing designers and gives them an understanding of what products will appeal to the public. If Venus is found in this decanate these qualities will be strengthened. There is a fondness for personal possessions that are well made, durable, of lasting value, and aesthetic appeal. These natives would rather have a few things of superior quality than many mediocre ones. Because of the fixed-sign nature of Taurus, their staying power and determination will be greater than that of other Virgos, who tire easily. They are also apt to be stronger and more physically robust.

Virgo Duads

0-2½° Virgo

The first duad of Virgo is the Virgo-Virgo or Mercury-Mercury duad. Because this duad is part of the Virgo-Mercury decanate of Virgo, the qualities ascribed to the sign Virgo and the first decanate of Virgo apply to this duad in an intensified manner. These natives are concerned with diet and health and are prone to experimentation with health food regimens. They are often talented in the healing arts or work related to health and hygiene. At times they can be shy and retiring, especially around strangers. Their job is the hub of the universe for these Virgos.

2½-5° Virgo

The second duad of Virgo is the Virgo-Libra or Mercury-Venus duad. These natives are more socially outgoing than the average shy Virgo. They prefer jobs in public relations or psychology, although their artistic ability makes them good clothing designers and creators of objects that are attractive as well as useful. They may show a literary talent in practical fields such as advertising, or in other kinds of writing. These natives seek to improve the work environment by beautifying the work area or establishing pleasant relationships with coworkers. They often attract romance through their work or their comings and goings. The manners, dress and personal hygiene of the people with whom they associate are very important to them. Even when not engaged in actually creating things that are both beautiful and functional, they know how to select them. They may spend considerable money on attractive clothing and personal items. These natives have the ability to make money, but alternate saving periods with spending sprees.

5-7½° Virgo
The third duad of Virgo is the Virgo-Scorpio or Mercury-Mars-Pluto duad. In general it can be said that this is a "no nonsense" duad. Those with it prominent in the horoscope have sharp, critical minds, and an exceptional ability to penetrate to the heart of any problem, especially in their work. They are gifted at devising new ways of solving problems and developing greater efficiency. Their insight into the motives and intentions of others results in comments and criticisms that are generally accurate, if not always charitable. When annoyed they can be caustic in their speech. These Virgos make excellent researchers and scientific investigators because of their unique ability to get to the bottom of mysteries. The fixed-sign nature of Scorpio gives them determination and follow through so that the tasks they undertake are done with thoroughness and precision. Since the intelligence of Mercury tempers the impulsiveness of Mars, these natives plan their actions in advance.

7½-10° Virgo
The fourth duad of Virgo is the Virgo-Sagittarius or Mercury-Jupiter duad. Those with this duad prominent in the horoscope are attracted to education, teaching, social work, and educating the public about health, hygiene, and apparel. They often become workers in educational, medical, religious, or social institutions, and for better or worse become indoctrinated by the way of life of the institutions they depend upon for their livelihood. Because Virgo and Sagittarius are both mutable signs, these natives are able to adapt to changing social conditions but do not always have the staying power of other Virgos. The philosophical understanding of Sagittarius, combined with the practicality of Virgo, gives these natives a balanced mental outlook. Little things in the environment give them important clues about the long-range trends of the culture to which they belong, and enable them to gain prophetic insights into the future.

10-12½° Virgo
The fifth duad of Virgo is the Virgo-Capricorn or Mercury-Saturn duad. Because this duad is part of the Capricorn decanate of Virgo, the qualities ascribed to the second decanate of Virgo apply to this duad in an intensified manner. Those with this duad prominent in the horoscope have intense professional ambition and an unvoiced desire to some day go into business for themselves. They are practical, ambitious and

hard-working, making good supervisors, production managers, and administrators. Their moral and social values tend toward the traditional and conservative outlook. They often are austere and reserved in personal mannerism and shy away from what they consider frivolous or meaningless social activities—that is, anything that will not lead to meaningful and lasting gains. These natives are often highly skilled in such areas as craftsmanship, mathematics, accounting, and scientific research requiring skill, patience, organization, and precision. The strong professional ambition of this duad leads many into medical careers. Because of the Mercury influence, professional responsibilities may necessitate considerable short-distance travel. The above-mentioned qualities will be more strongly marked if Saturn is found in this duad.

12½-15° Virgo
The sixth duad of Virgo is the Virgo-Aquarius or Mercury-Uranus duad. Those with this duad prominent in the horoscope have strong scientific and intellectual abilities because of the double-Saturn, double-Mercury influence. (Mercury rules Virgo and is exalted in Aquarius. Saturn rules the decanate to which this duad belongs, and co-rules Aquarius.) These double influences combine with Virgo's practicality and the Uranus influence of Aquarius to give these natives a kind of intuitive inspiration, an originality of thought, and the skills needed to implement their ideas in a practical way. They are especially talented in such fields as writing, engineering, technology, mathematics, and scientific research. Because of the group orientation of Aquarius, these natives often become organizers and leaders of union activities and practical scientific or humanitarian group endeavors. They often establish friendships through their work and acquire knowledge through practical experimentation. Much of their work is carried on in cooperation with others. There is an ability for spiritual healing and an interest in non-drug healing methods.

15-17½° Virgo
The seventh duad of Virgo is the Virgo-Pisces or Mercury-Jupiter-Neptune duad. Those having this duad prominent in the horoscope often have intuitive or psychic abilities that enable them to diagnose or cure illness by spiritual means. Much of this intuitive knowledge comes from the native's subconscious past experience, which also enables him or her to penetrate into the workings of karmic law. Since this duad is part of the Capricorn decanate, these natives are often saddled with the responsibility of straightening out and taking care of people who are emotionally, psychologically, or mentally ill and disoriented. They frequently work in connection with hospitals or institutions. These Virgos can become depressed if overworked, and should guard against being psychically

drained by the negative conditions of people around them. Fortunately, because of the Saturn decanate's influence and Neptune's intuitive capacity, they have the ability to hold the mind steady and go deeply into meditation.

17½-20° Virgo

The eighth duad of Virgo is the Virgo-Aries or Mercury-Mars duad. These natives have sharp, critical minds, much as do those who have the Virgo-Scorpio duad prominent in the horoscope. Because this duad is part of the Capricorn decanate of Virgo, there is a double-cardinal and double-Mars influence that inclines them toward forceful, decisive action. Because of the Mercury and Saturn influence they are capable of planning their actions beforehand. These natives are especially talented in such fields as engineering and mechanical design. They have competitive and ambitious minds and are fond of debates and contests, especially in their work or business. They are resourceful in solving problems related to their work or business. They are also resourceful in solving problems related to their work by finding new ways to do the job. When annoyed they can be caustic in their remarks. These Virgos like programs of sports, calisthenics, yoga, or other forms of physical exercise as a means of improving health. The qualities of this duad are more strongly marked if Mars is located here.

20-22½° Virgo

The ninth duad of Virgo is the Virgo-Taurus or Mercury-Venus duad. Because this duad is part of the Taurus decanate of Virgo, the qualities ascribed to the third decanate of Virgo apply to this duad in an intensified manner. The double-Venus influence gives these natives a strong sense of beauty and refinement. Like the second duad of Virgo, they prefer harmonious surroundings in the work area. Business people with this duad prominent are usually impeccably dressed in order to impress their clients and gain an aura of reliability and status. Creature comforts and objects that represent status give them a sense of security and importance in their job. Since the Moon is exalted in Taurus, these natives are fond of good food, clothing, and creature comforts. They lavish attention and work on their family and home, and are concerned with their family's health, diet, and status. These Virgos have a strong, practical business sense that make them good managers, accountants, and sales people, especially in areas related to art, music, luxury items, clothing, gourmet foods, health, and beauty aids.

22½-25° Virgo

The tenth duad of Virgo is the Virgo-Gemini or Mercury-Mercury duad. Because of the double Mercury influence, these natives are highly intelligent and even more so if Mercury is located here. They are gifted in such fields as teaching, lecturing, editing, administrative work, mathematics, science, drafting, and engineering design. They make good writers, especially on such subjects as health, food, clothing, art, and hygiene. In -general they combine insight into theory with practical experience and know-how. There can be ability in graphic arts because of the Venus connotation. This often involves work with charts, diagrams, and graphic illustrations. There can be skill in such fields as advertising and public relations, especially through the printed word. Since Gemini and Virgo are both mutable signs, natives of this duad have delicate nervous systems and need adequate rest and proper diet to function at their best. They must discipline themselves to follow through on projects they start because there can be a tendency to scatter their energy. Because this duad is part of the Taurus decanate of Virgo, they can persevere. These natives have a pleasing and harmonious manner of speech and communication.

25-27½° Virgo
The eleventh duad of Virgo is the Virgo-Cancer or Mercury-Moon duad. There is a double-Moon influence (intensified if the Moon is located here) because the Moon rules Cancer and is exalted in Taurus, the decanate to which this duad belongs. As a result, these natives make exceptional cooks and homemakers. They are often associated with restaurants, the food industry, or dietary concerns, and they have a special talent for businesses related to food, farming, or domestic products and services. These Virgos are especially concerned about orderliness and cleanliness of the home and family, and about money to provide family security. They often have deep-rooted attitudes as a result of their early upbringing and past conditioning.

27½-30° Virgo
This is the Virgo-Leo or Mercury-Sun duad. These natives have a greater vitality than the average Virgo due to the fixed-fire influence of Leo. Because of the Leo duad and the Taurus decanate combination, they can display surprising determination and staying power, as well as the ability to express themselves in an artistic and creative way. This duad often produces skilled artisans of various types. These natives make excellent teachers or workers with young people. Since they are inclined to assume positions of leadership and authority, they do not remain in subordinate positions for long. They like to dramatize their work or profession. They have the ability to influence the attitudes of others in subtle ways. They can be authoritative about details and see that those who work under them do not neglect small but important matters. They also have the ability to inspire others with greater enthusiasm in the performance of their tasks.

Libra

Libra

Sign: Libra   **Ruler:** Venus

Libra Decanate 1: 0-10° Libra   Ruler: Venus

Libra Decanate 1 Duads:

| 0-2½° Libra | 2½-5° Scorpio | 5-7½° Sagittarius | 7½-10° Capricorn |
| Ruler: Venus | Rulers: Mars, Pluto | Ruler: Jupiter | Ruler: Saturn |

Libra Decanate 2: 10-20° Aquarius   Ruler: Uranus

Libra Decanate 2 Duads:

10-12½° Aquarius   12½-15° Pisces   15-17½° Aries   17½-20° Taurus
Ruler: Uranus,   Rulers: Jupiter,   Rulers: Mars   Ruler: Venus
   Saturn   Neptune   Pluto

Libra Decanate 3: 20-30° Gemini   Ruler: Mercury

Libra Decanate 3 Duads:

20-22½° Gemini   22½-25° Cancer   25-27½° Leo   27½-30° Virgo
Ruler: Mercury   Ruler: Moon   Ruler: Sun   Ruler: Mercury

Libra

The sign Libra is of the air triplicity. Hence, those with this sign prominent in the horoscope are concerned with the intellectual affairs of life. Unlike Gemini, however, their primary interest is in human psychology rather than ideas and information per se.

Likewise, Libra's nature as a positive-masculine sign of the cardinal quadruplicity confers those of its temperament with the ability to initiate social activity, spurring them to establish interpersonal relationships and partnerships. These individuals need not await the responses of others before taking affirmative action, as is characteristic of Cancer.

Those with Libra prominent find meaning for their lives in the sharing of experiences with others. Though this is largely a reaction to the loneliness and drudgery associated with the Virgo phase of their evolutionary development, it gives them an acute awareness of the intentions and responses of others. Marriage and other forms of partnership are of primary importance in the lives of these natives.

Saturn's exaltation in Libra imparts a sense of justice, responsibility and reliable conduct to all relationships of importance to individuals of this temperament, and because of this, many of these natives are attracted to the legal profession. Venus' rulership of Libra likewise endows those of Libra temperament with a strong sense of refinement in art, music, personal appearance and conduct. Uncouth behavior or crude surroundings are objectionable to them. These natives can accept simplicity, but not ugliness.

Libra Decanates

0-10° Libra
The first decanate of Libra is the Libra-Libra or Venus-Venus decanate. These natives wish to attract a beautiful and comfortable environment. They have refined tastes and need harmonious surroundings in which to carry out their functions. They are socially and artistically inclined. Because they are entering into the second half of the zodiac, which deals with human relationships, these natives are concerned with how other people act and are eager to enter into relationships and establish partnerships. But they must be careful about acquiescing to the attitudes and actions of others merely for the sake of popularity and acceptance. As a rule, Libras with a strong Saturn in the horoscope are not subject to this danger because of their strong principles. These natives are attracted to the study of psychology and the social sciences. They have a strong need to receive and express love, so marriage is of paramount importance in their lives.

10-20° Libra
The second decanate of Libra is the Libra-Aquarius or Venus-Saturn-Uranus decanate. There is a double-Saturn influence in this decanate because Saturn is exalted in Libra and co-rules Aquarius. According to Alice Bailey's esoteric astrology, Uranus is also the esoteric ruler of Libra. Because Uranus also rules Aquarius, its influence is very strong in this decanate. Natives with this decanate prominent possess unusual intuitive faculties, as well as good organization and the capacity for self-discipline. Because of Libra's concern with relationships, they have an excellent understanding of karmic law and principles of justice. For these reasons, these natives make excellent lawyers, judges, arbitrators, and negotiators. They often meet close friends and partners in unusual and unexpected ways. They have unusual friendships with people of all ages and walks of life. Those under this decanate are often associated with groups and organizations. These natives can have a scientific turn of mind which can unfold in an interest in electronics or an occult study such as astrology. Because Aquarius is a fixed sign, these natives have more perseverance than Libras of other decanates.

20-30° Libra
The third decanate of Libra is the Libra-Gemini or Venus-Mercury decanate. These natives often have literary abilities, especially in such fields such as advertising, publicity, poetry, art, music, criticism, or other pursuits related to the arts. There is also much short-distance travel in connection with social activities, business, and possibly such things as lecturing. Because of the Gemini influence these natives can be inconsistent or

fickle in romantic relationships and friendships. They prefer variety and do not want to be exclusively tied down to one relationship. They are able to adapt to many different social situations and to different types of people. Monotonous routine or a humdrum existence tends to bore them. The mutable-cardinal combination inherent in this decanate means they must discipline themselves to follow through on the things they initiate.

Libra Duads

0-2½° Libra

The first duad of Libra is the Libra-Libra or Venus-Venus duad. Because this duad is part of the Libra-Venus decanate of Libra, the qualities ascribed to the sign Libra and the first decanate of Libra apply to this duad in an intensified manner. If Venus is found in this duad the native will have exceptional social sensitivity, musical ability, and artistic talent. Venus in this duad often confers physical beauty and grace, especially in women.

2½-5° Libra

The second duad of Libra is the Libra-Scorpio or Venus-Mars-Pluto duad. These natives are known as the Libras who have an iron hand in a velvet glove. Saturn exalted in Libra combines with the Mars-Pluto rulership of Scorpio to give them surprising toughness and tenacity, even while expressing typical Libra charm and diplomacy. Since there is skill in cooperative business enterprises and corporate affairs they make good fund-raisers, negotiators, and public relations people for corporate enterprises. They also have skill in business matters related to arts and crafts and insights on how to make money off these endeavors. Because of the Mars-Venus-Pluto combination these natives are highly sexed. They can be passionate—and sometimes jealous—in love relationships, especially if Mars or Venus is located here.

5-7½° Libra

The third duad of Libra is the Libra-Sagittarius or Venus-Jupiter duad. Those with this duad prominent in the horoscope have generous, sociable, outgoing personalities. They make good promoters and public relations representatives for religious, educational, charitable, and cultural organizations and institutions. There can also be long-distance travel in pursuit of education related to art, music, religion, and cultural history. These natives have a desire to exemplify whatever ethical standards they adopt as their personal philosophy. They are kind, sympathetic, and considerate toward others because of the combined Neptune-Jupiter-Venus influence. This does not guarantee practicality, but the natives generally mean well despite a possible tendency toward laziness and taking too much for granted. Their desire to help others is often expressed through charitable work. These Libras are endowed with creative, imaginative qualities, and have a preference for classical and religious forms of art and music. They can have intuitive and prophetic insights into the reactions and feelings of others and the future course of relationships.

7½-10° Libra

The fourth duad of Libra is the Libra-Capricorn or Venus-Saturn duad. There is a double-Saturn influence in this duad because Saturn is exalted in Libra and rules Capricorn. Those with this duad prominent in the horoscope are more serious, practical, and reserved than the average Libra. They have a strict sense of justice, fair play, and discipline in business and professional affairs. Many natives are attracted to the legal profession. Because of the Capricorn influence they do have strong professional ambitions, and because Mars is exalted in Capricorn they can be more aggressive than other Libras. Both Libra and Capricorn are cardinal signs, so these natives are capable of energetic, decisive action whenever necessary; but it is usually preceded by a careful weighing and balancing of the effects of any decision they make. They can be effective as political strategists because they are astute in anticipating the reactions of others. As artists they have a strong sense of structure and composition in their work. In social relations they have a strong sense of propriety, manners, and proper conduct that makes them more formal in relationships than other Libras.

10-12½° Libra

The fifth duad of Libra is the Libra-Aquarius or Venus-Saturn-Uranus duad. Because this duad is part of the Aquarius decanate of Libra the qualities ascribed to the second decanate of Libra apply to this duad in an intensified manner. Since Libra and Aquarius are both air signs, those with this duad prominent in the horoscope have strong intellectual characteristics. There is a triple-Saturn influence resulting from Saturn's exaltation in Libra and co-rulership of the Aquarius decanate and duad. Therefore, these natives are good organizers of interpersonal, group, and business dealings. Because of the Mercury and Uranus influence of Aquarius these natives have original minds and scientific or mathematical ability. They are subject to sudden flashes of intuitive understanding that gives them insight into superphysical realms as well as solutions to practical problems. There can be ability in writing, scientific research, engineering, and large-scale humanitarian projects and organizational endeavors.

12½-15° Libra

The sixth duad of Libra is the Libra-Pisces or Venus-Neptune-Jupiter duad. Those with this duad prominent have excellent intuitive abilities, especially regarding people and human relations, because of the influence of Uranus and Neptune. (Neptune rules Pisces, and Uranus rules the Aquarius decanate to which this duad belongs.) There is emotional sensitivity because Pisces is a water sign, and intellectuality because Libra and Aquarius are both air signs. Venus is exalted in Pisces and rules Libra, giving a double-Venus influence to this duad and endowing these natives with refined judgment and creative artistic ability. They are capable of great charm and diplomacy, sympathy, and understanding, while at the same time maintaining an impartial and objective viewpoint. These abilities stem from the influence of Saturn, Uranus, and Mercury in the Aquarius decanate to which this duad belongs. Libra is a cardinal sign, Aquarius is a fixed sign, and Pisces is mutable, giving this duad a good balance of initiatives, determination, and adaptability. These natives can be successful in businesses related to art, music, entertainment, and public relations where aesthetic and social sensitivity must be combined with practical business sense and good timing. The combined Mercury, Neptune, and Saturn influence can give the ability for writing and public speaking.

15-17½° Libra

The seventh duad of Libra is the Libra-Aries or Venus-Mars duad. Those with this duad prominent are more aggressive, competitive and self-assertive than the average Libra. Because Libra and Aries are both cardinal signs and Mars rules Aries, these natives are capable of decisive action. Those with planets in this duad are concerned about what others think of them, and may be intellectually competitive. Because of the Mars-Pluto influence of Aries and the Uranus influence of the Aquarius decanate, there is an independent manner of thinking and acting. These natives will cooperate with others, but they refuse to be ordered or coerced by them. They have a progressive interest in advanced ways of doing things that makes them like to be first in discovering and applying new ideas. Because of Saturn's influence these natives are capable of exerting great willpower in putting their ideas into action. They are capable of revamping and regenerating old friendships and partnerships, and can be aggressive in initiating joint partnerships and corporate ventures. Because of the Mars-Venus-Uranus-Pluto combination inherent in this duad these natives can have a strong sex drive.

17½-20° Libra

The eighth duad of Libra is the Libra-Taurus or Venus-Venus duad. Those with this duad prominent in the horoscope have marked artistic abilities because of the double-Venus influence, and can be involved with music, painting, sculpture, or business activities related to the arts especially if Venus is found here. Since this duad is part of the Aquarius decanate, and since Taurus and Aquarius are both fixed signs, these natives can have considerable determination and staying power, and typically are physically robust—more so than the average Libra. These natives can be sensuous, and they enjoy the good creature comforts of life, but if carried too far these preferences may result in plain laziness. These individuals are inclined toward business and practical money-making endeavors, and are especially attracted to sales and public relations because of the practical nature of Taurus, the diplomatic nature of Libra, and the determination of Taurus and Aquarius.

20-22½° Libra
The ninth duad of Libra is the Libra-Gemini or Venus-Mercury duad. Because this duad is part of the Gemini decanate of Libra, the qualities ascribed to the third decanate of Libra apply this duad in an intensified manner. Those with this duad prominent have intellectual and literary ability, and often there is a talent for graphic art. These natives have pleasant speech, a charming manner, and make excellent writers or speakers on artistic and musical subjects. They can be good at writing poetry and stories, or doing other creative literary work. There is tremendous curiosity concerning human relationships, psychology, and personal interactions, but it might be expressed as a tendency to gossip. These natives often have close ties with brothers, sisters, neighbors, and intellectual acquaintances. There will be much coming and going related to social activities, partnerships, romance, and marriage.

22½-25° Libra
The tenth duad of Libra is the Libra-Cancer or Venus-Moon duad. Those with this duad prominent have close emotional ties with their families. They are consciously or unconsciously motivated to marriage as a means of establishing a home and family, which in turn will provide them with emotional and material security. These natives are generally sympathetic and kind toward family members, and because this duad is part of the Gemini decanate of Libra, are frequently in communication with them. Business partnership activities are often carried on in the home, and these partnerships often involve family members. The natives also like to host social events in the home, which they make a showplace for art, music, and literature. Men with this duad prominent have a special knack for getting along with women and understanding their moods and psychology. These individuals often make good cooks who make their food attractive to the eye as well as to the palate.

25-27½° Libra

The eleventh duad of Libra is the Libra-Leo or Venus-Sun duad. Libra is a cardinal sign, the Gemini decanate has a mutable influence, and the Leo duad brings a fixed sign quality, so there is a good balance of cardinal, mutable, and fixed influences in this duad. These natives can express themselves through the performing arts, music, entertainment, or art. They have a great self-confidence, and a dramatic flair in meeting the public or impressing others with their grace and charm. They make good public relations people and promoters since their Libra diplomacy is combined with Leo's self-confidence and Gemini's dexterity in speech. They can express their ideas with authority, and usually win others over to their point of view. There is a special talent for sparking social gatherings and arousing enthusiasm in others.

27½-30° Libra

The twelfth duad of Libra is the Libra-Virgo or Venus-Mercury duad. Because this duad is part of the Gemini decanate, also ruled by Mercury, there will be strong practical and intellectual traits. Those with this duad prominent are very adaptable in social situations and skillful in social and business communication. They are often talented in such fields as advertising and illustration, and make skillful literary critics and commentators. Harmonious relationships and beautiful surroundings are important to the work and health of these natives. They have strong interest in clothing, attractive dress, and personal hygiene. Often they are interested in health regimens as a means of improving personal attractiveness and appeal to the opposite sex. These Libras often have friendships and partnerships arising out of their work, and sometimes meet their marriage partner in this way.

Scorpio

Scorpio

Sign: Scorpio   **Rulers:** Pluto, Mars

Scorpio Decanate 1: 0-10° Scorpio   Rulers: Pluto, Mars

Scorpio Decanate 1 Duads:

0-2½° Scorpio	2½-5° Sagittarius	5-7½° Capricorn	7½-10° Aquarius
Rulers: Pluto, Mars	Ruler: Jupiter	Ruler: Saturn	Rulers: Uranus, Saturn

Scorpio Decanate 2: 10-20° Pisces   Rulers: Jupiter, Neptune

Scorpio Decanate 2 Duads:

10-12½° Pisces	12½-15° Aries	15-17½° Taurus	17½-20° Gemini
Rulers: Jupiter, Neptune	Rulers: Mars, Pluto	Ruler: Venus	Ruler: Mercury

Scorpio Decanate 3: 20-30° Cancer   Ruler: Moon

Scorpio Decanate 3 Duads:

20-22½° Cancer	22½-25° Leo	25-27½° Virgo	27½-30° Libra
Ruler: Moon	Ruler: Sun	Ruler: Mercury	Ruler: Venus

Scorpio

Scorpio's placement in the water triplicity confers a highly-charged emotional nature. These natives feel intensely about life and their place within it. Its added nature as a fixed sign causes these individuals to lack the ability to change or adapt their emotional attitudes as easily as other water signs. Thus, whatever emotional attitude they may entertain will be followed relentlessly to its final conclusion, whether it be positive or negative, culminating in the achievement of great heights or personal degradation. This is why it is said of Scorpio that this sign produces both the highest and lowest examples of human expression. This is also why it is so important for natives of the Scorpio disposition to choose constructive paths from the very beginning, for once they have entered upon a way of life, it is not easily changed.

Even though it is ruled by the dynamic planets Mars and Pluto, Scorpio is a negative-feminine sign. Thus, individuals of its temperament can irrevocably change and transform that which is around them, for better or worse. Always, however, this must be accomplished within the context of existing conditions and circumstances. Although these natives may not be able to choose the situations that confront them, they do possess the power to transform them into a higher or lower form of expression. Hence, those with Scorpio prominent are always trying to improve the status quo.

Uranus' exaltation in this sign, combined with Pluto's rulership of it, gives these natives strong psychic abilities and the potential for developing occult powers, leading to the ability to transform or transmute to a higher level of expression that which they touch.

Those of Scorpio temperament are thorough, and masters at detailed perfection, due largely to their ability to comprehend and understand the underlying causes behind things.

Scorpio Decanates

0-10° Scorpio

The first decanate of Scorpio is the Scorpio-Scorpio or Mars-Pluto-Mars-Pluto decanate. Those with this decanate prominent in the horoscope have intense emotions and are capable of exercising great willpower. These natives have a special ability to find resourceful ways of utilizing old and discarded things. Consciously or unconsciously, they understand that all manifested things are an expression of energy and that energy is not lost but merely takes another form.

They know that everything around them can be used as it is or transformed into something else that can be used; otherwise it wouldn't be in existence to begin with. Because of this understanding, these natives have little fear of change or death, recognizing these forces as part of an on-going evolutionary process leading to ever-greater expansion of consciousness and the creation of perfection.

These Scorpios are highly enterprising in business, manufacturing, engineering, and scientific investigation. They possess great energy and have the tenacity to succeed even against great obstacles. They have little tolerance for weakness and laziness in others, and will not permit it in themselves. Nor are they easily deterred by threats or attempts to instill fear or thoughts of failure into them. Often there is a do-or-die attitude that can be very uncompromising, and they can make determined, sometimes vindictive, enemies, which can be very uncomfortable for those who incur their displeasure but is equally destructive to the native who nurses resentments.

This decanate has a strong sex drive and its natives are capable of being jealous and possessive of sexual partners. They are not always charitable in forgiving the oversights or weaknesses of others, especially if their pride is hurt. They can be cold and indifferent to those they consider beneath their dignity, and their speech is guarded, tending to be secretive—especially with information that has some strategic importance.

Joint finances and corporate financial dealings are often important in the lives of these Scorpios.

10-20° Scorpio

The second decanate of Scorpio is the Scorpio-Pisces or Mars-Pluto-Jupiter-Neptune decanate. These natives are more kind and sympathetic than the usual Scorpio because of the Pisces influence. They will help those in need, but are sufficiently Scorpio to expect others to help themselves after that. If it doesn't happen, they become annoyed, upset, and indifferent the next time around.

Because of the Neptune, Uranus, and Pluto influences, these native can have strongly intuitive abilities and are often drawn to mysticism, occultism, or magic. They are especially interested in such things as reincarnation and life after death. Uri Geller has the Moon, Venus, and Jupiter in this decanate, an example of the occult powers it confers. If Neptune, Uranus, Pluto, Jupiter, or Venus is located here, the psychic abilities conferred by this decanate are increased.

20-30° Scorpio

The third decanate of Scorpio is the Scorpio-Cancer or Mars-Pluto-Moon decanate. Because Neptune and Jupiter are exalted in Cancer, there are many similarities with the second Pisces decanate of Scorpio where these planets also rule. These natives have strong intuitive tendencies because of the combination of Neptune, Pluto, and Uranus influences, but are more decisive than individuals of the second decanate of Scorpio because Cancer is a cardinal sign.

Those with this decanate prominent are concerned with home improvement and family affairs. They can be emotionally sensitive and easily hurt—more than is apparent—especially in regard to family relationships. These natives can be moody, subject to rapid emotional changes, and liable to act on impulse because of Mars' rulership of Scorpio combined with the Moon influence. They are often interested in psychic communication with deceased relatives. If any of the planets located here are afflicted, there may be conflicts within the family over inheritance, alimony, or goods belonging to the dead, or possibly disputes over the jurisdiction of children in divorce cases.

Scorpio Duads

0-2½° Scorpio

The first duad of Scorpio is the Scorpio-Scorpio or Mars-Pluto-Mars-Pluto duad. Because this duad is part of the Scorpio decanate of Scorpio, the qualities ascribed to the sign Scorpio and the first decanate of Scorpio apply to this duad in an intensified manner. Those with this duad prominent are just entering into the Scorpio experience. They have fresh energy and zeal to dare great things. At the same time they may neglect some of the amenities of kindness and consideration toward others. These softer qualities are combined with the Scorpio nature later in the second and third decanates, usually as the result of harsh experiences. In reaction to the seeming compromise and indecisiveness of the previous sign, Libra, these natives are out to reform and transform whatever is around them. They are capable of intense willpower and strong dedication to the causes they espouse. Many are attracted to the military or police professions. They feel they can do a job better and more efficiently than others—and in many cases they are right.

2½-5° Scorpio

The second duad of Scorpio is the Scorpio-Sagittarius or Mars-Pluto-Neptune-Jupiter duad. Those with this duad prominent in the horoscope often become crusaders for some religious, educational, philosophic, or cultural cause, especially in fund-raising and administrative capacities. When they feel morally justified in what they are doing they can be relentless in pursuing a goal. This does not mean that they are without ethics, only that their sense of ethics can have blind spots and that they run the danger of believing might makes right. These natives are enthusiastic about their work and can inspire confidence and enthusiasm in others. There is an honest attempt to apply their philosophy in action. They may work hard to establish industrial systems or means of employment for others whereby they can help themselves in an honorable way. Their considerable vision and foresight combined with Scorpio resourcefulness enables them to prepare effectively for the future. In fact, their insight into the future can be clairvoyant in nature because of the Neptune influence of Sagittarius and the Uranus-Pluto influence of Scorpio.

5-7° Scorpio

The third duad of Scorpio is the Scorpio-Capricorn or Mars-Pluto-Saturn duad. Those with this duad prominent in the horoscope often possess strong administrative talent. The double-Mars influence resulting from Mars' exaltation in Capricorn and rulership of Scorpio gives them a capacity for decisive, energetic, organized action. Their resourceful and disciplined thoroughness makes them well suited for positions of leadership and responsibility. They know how to make use of available resources, how to take charge, and how to get things done. These natives are highly ambitious and often rise to a position of prominence in their chosen field. These Scorpios may be stern disciplinarians, and sometimes harsh, old and unsympathetic. They generally do not forgive slothfulness, inefficiency, or lack of attention to duty, but their standards for themselves are more stringent than for others. It is important that these natives maintain a spiritual philosophy because if their desire for power is directed in a ruthless and purely materialistic way that sacrifices human values, the result is pain and unhappiness for all concerned.

7½-10° Scorpio

The fourth duad of Scorpio is the Scorpio-Aquarius or Mars-Pluto-Uranus-Saturn duad. Because Uranus is exalted in Scorpio and the Scorpio decanate, and rules Aquarius, there is a triple-Uranus influence in this duad, making these natives independent, resourceful, innovative, scientifically oriented, and often involved with the occult. Saturn's influence in Aquarius gives these natives good organizational ability to go with Scorpio's thoroughness and resourcefulness. Often there is special engineering and scientific ability with this duad. Since Aquarius is an air sign these natives are able to be more detached and objective concerning emotional issues than the average Scorpio. They can be friendly, communicative and socially outgoing. The strong Uranus influence shows a daring love of adventure and unusual, exciting experiences that could result in recklessness and personal danger if carried to excess.

10-12½° Scorpio

The fifth duad of Scorpio is the Scorpio-Pisces or Mars-Pluto-Jupiter-Neptune duad. Because this duad is part of the Pisces decanate of Scorpio, the qualities ascribed to the second decanate of Scorpio apply to this duad in an intensified manner. These natives are more emotionally sensitive and softhearted than the average Scorpio. Because of the combined influence of Uranus, Pluto, and Neptune, they have strong imaginative and intuitive faculties and can be unusually clairvoyant, as can natives of the second decanate as a whole. They have an interest in occult and mystical pursuits and can be excellent spiritual healers. These natives can have intense emotional reactions when subconscious memories are activated by present experiences, which makes their behavior strange and incomprehensible. They often have keen insights into the motivations of others, but can be easily taken in by appeals for help, later resenting it if those they assist do not also do something to help themselves. These people have an extremely wide understanding of life and what is expected in the living of it. An interest in creative artistic expression involving the improvement and renovation of old things could give a special knack for the restoration of art objects and might be financially rewarding.

12½-15° Scorpio

The sixth duad of Scorpio is the Scorpio-Aries or Mars-Pluto-Mars-Pluto duad. Those with this duad prominent in the horoscope are more energetic and aggressive in their approach to life than the average Scorpio because of the double Mars-Pluto emphasis. They are often attracted to military or police careers, and make aggressive entrepreneurs and industrialists because of their immense self-confidence and willpower, enough to let them tackle a project even against seemingly insurmountable odds. There is tremendous vitality and energy that can be used to transform existing conditions and accomplish great feats of strength and psychic concentration, but a might makes right attitude can be a danger for these natives. They must be careful not to infringe on the rights of others with less strength or power. Because of the double-Mars influence they have the strength to act decisively, and since they are unmovable in defense of what they consider to be right, attempts to intimidate or coerce them simply make them all the more determined to pursue their own course of action.

15-17½° Scorpio

The seventh duad of Scorpio is the Scorpio-Taurus or Mars-Pluto-Venus duad. Because Taurus and Scorpio are business-oriented signs, these natives are often attracted to careers involving corporations, banking, insurance, investments, industry, and the management of other people's money. There is great perseverance, patience, and determination to succeed in business, industrial, and professional endeavors as a result of the double fixed-sign influence. They can excel in businesses related to art and the restoration of valuable property. The combination of Mars, Pluto, and Venus gives these natives a strong sex drive and a sensual side to their nature that may result in extreme sexual jealousy and possessiveness. They desire luxury, status, and creature comforts, often acquiring costly possessions of beauty, luxury, and elegance. These natives should be careful not to make money their primary objective in life, or they will end up being owned by their possessions, caught in an exhausting and never-ending materialist race.

17½-20° Scorpio

The eighth duad of Scorpio is the Scorpio-Gemini or Mars-Pluto-Mercury duad. Those with this duad prominent have keen, penetrating, investigative minds that enable them to solve problems and understand scientific and occult mysteries. Much valuable information comes to them through intuitive channels and they may be able to transmit healing energy through their hands. The speech of these natives is to the point, incisive, and succinct. If used correctly it can inspire and illuminate the minds of others, but it may also result in cutting sarcasm. Because Gemini and Pisces are mutable signs, these Scorpios are much more versatile than average. They can be effective in mystery writing, economic analysis, occultism, and science.

20-22½° Scorpio

The ninth duad of Scorpio is the Scorpio-Cancer or Mars-Pluto-Moon duad. Because this duad is part of the Cancer decanate of Scorpio, the qualities ascribed to the third decanate of Scorpio apply to this duad in an intensified manner. Those with this duad prominent are often attracted to real estate, farming, and businesses related to food commodities as a means of providing for the future security of home and family—matters of chief importance to these natives. Like the fifth duad of Scorpio, they are emotionally sensitive and may have considerable occult abilities. These natives are strongly patriotic and emotional in their political and religious philosophy, sometimes to the point of fanaticism. Their strong subconscious emotional attitudes are based on family conditioning and early childhood experiences, or conditioning related to previous embodiments and subconscious telepathic influences. It is different from the Neptune conditioning, although the two are closely related because Jupiter and Neptune are exalted in Cancer and because family conditions originate either in karmic causes or the necessity of rounding out undeveloped areas in the evolution of these natives.

22½-25° Scorpio

The tenth duad of Scorpio is the Scorpio-Leo or Mars-Pluto-Sun duad. These natives are determined and persevering because Leo and Scorpio are both fixed signs. The double-Pluto influence of this duad (originating in Pluto's rulership of Scorpio and exaltation in Leo) gives these natives a powerful and relentless will. They often attain positions of power and leadership in their chosen fields because of their well-developed powers of resourcefulness, thoroughness, endurance, self-confidence, and personal magnetism. This duad often involves the native in corporate financial dealings. These natives have great creative power in business and industry, and an ability to improve existing conditions that can result in the creative use of their inherent spiritual willpower and one-pointed concentration. They must avoid an attitude of personal superiority because it will alienate those who could assist them in attaining their objectives.

25-27½° Scorpio

The eleventh duad of Scorpio is the Scorpio-Virgo or Mars-Pluto-Mercury duad. Scorpio is a fixed sign, Virgo is mutable, and the Cancer decanate adds a cardinal influence, so there is good blend of decisiveness, determination, and adaptability in this duad. These natives are practical and resourceful in their work. There is often a strong interest in healing, including the use of meditation, laying-on of hands, massage, and the utilization of spiritual energies. There can be an innovative use of clothing and an interest in personal dress. Women with this duad prominent combine Scorpio mystique with Virgo style, an unbeatable combination as far as personal appearance is concerned. Because of the analytical mental ability of Virgo and Scorpio's resourcefulness, depth, and insight, these natives make excellent scientific researchers, engineers, and business analysts. They are good critics, but not always charitable in what they have to say. They can be sarcastic and cutting in their remarks, but also observe accurately and have a deep appreciation for quality work.

27½-30° Scorpio
The twelfth duad of Scorpio is the Scorpio-Libra or Mars-Pluto-Venus duad. Those with this duad prominent in the horoscope have a strong tendency to want to mold and remake close friends, marriage partners, and those with whom they have business relations, which can cause resentment if not done with tact and diplomacy. This duad can give innovative and creative abilities in such fields as art and entertainment. These natives often have talent in public relations associated with corporate business enterprises. They also have a knack for winning others over to their point of view and to the goals they espouse. Because of the Mars-Pluto-Venus combination, there is a strong sex drive and the danger of sexual jealousy.

Sagittarius

Sagittarius

Sign: Sagittarius   **Ruler:** Jupiter

Sagittarius Decanate 1: 0-10° Sagittarius   Ruler: Jupiter

Sagittarius Decanate 1 Duads:

0-2½° Sagittarius	2½-5° Capricorn	5-7½° Aquarius	7½-10° Pisces
Ruler: Jupiter	Ruler: Saturn	Rulers: Uranus, Saturn	Rulers: Jupiter, Neptune

Sagittarius Decanate 2: 10-20° Aries   Ruler: Mars

Sagittarius Decanate 2 Duads:

10-12½° Aries	12½-15° Taurus	15-17½° Gemini	17½-20° Cancer
Ruler: Mars	Ruler: Venus	Ruler: Mercury	Ruler: Moon

Sagittarius Decanate 3: 20-30° Leo   Ruler: Sun

Sagittarius Decanate 3 Duads:

20-22½° Leo	22½-25° Virgo	25-27½° Libra	27½-30° Scorpio
Ruler: Sun	Ruler: Mercury	Ruler: Venus	Rulers: Pluto, Mars

Sagittarius

Sagittarius' placement in the fire triplicity confers those of its temperament with energetic, creative, inspirational natures. Likewise, its membership in the mutable quadruplicity inclines these individuals to express their leadership potential and creative drive in and through their understanding of the history and development of the existing cultural institutions. All mutable signs draw upon past experience as a basis for activity, and those of the Sagittarian disposition make use of their cultural experience and insight to mold religious, ethical, educational, and cultural opinions and processes by directly influencing cultural ideologies.

These natives are less concerned with details and specific acts, in contrast to those exhibiting the mutable characteristics of Virgo and Gemini. Their interest, knowledge and expertise is of a more encompassing, though general, nature. Thus, they express their leadership abilities in a wider context, noticeably different from those of Aries or Leo, who express their potential through individual direct action or establishing themselves as a central authority figure. Care should be exercised, however, to avoid impractical ivory-tower approaches to life should this generalizing be carried to extremes.

The rulership of Sagittarius by Jupiter endows those of a Sagittarian temperament with intuitive insight and prophetic vision in the understanding of the future development of cultural institutions and attitudes. Boundless optimism will not permit these natives to concede to failure and because of this they often achieve great heights and inspire confidence in others.

Sagittarius Decanates

0-10° Sagittarius

The first decanate of Sagittarius is the Sagittarius-Sagittarius or Jupiter-Jupiter decanate. Those with this decanate prominent in the horoscope have an expansive, philosophical outlook and are interested in religion, philosophy, higher education, and the prevailing social order. There may be intuitive prophetic insights into future cultural developments. These natives are fond of travel and have a strong interest in foreign countries and their cultures, history, and religions. They continually set new goals for themselves to aspire to in the future. Because of their optimism they do not admit failure or become disheartened by difficulties, so they run the risk of overreaching themselves, neglecting important details, or making commitments that are impossible to fulfill. These Sagittarians often further their own ambitions by becoming ensconced in religious, cultural, or educational institutions, or by helping to promote large-scale projects in such areas.

10° to 20° Sagittarius

The second decanate of Sagittarius is the Sagittarius-Aries or Jupiter-Jupiter-Mars-Mars decanate, These natives are often militant crusaders for their particular religious, cultural, political, or educational beliefs, which can run the entire gamut of the religious and philosophic spectrum. Regardless of what their beliefs are, they promote and proselytize for them with militant, or even fanatic, zeal. They can easily go too far and annoy or alienate others. Because Jupiter is exalted in Cancer, sign of the home and homeland, there is also the danger of militaristic and narrowminded patriotic views based on the native's family background and cultural conditioning. On the other hand, they are able to initiate and spearhead worthwhile religious, cultural, or educational projects. These natives are fond of adventure and excitement and are likely to travel as a means of experiencing new adventures and thrilling experiences. This is a powerful decanate, providing the native with optimism, drive, initiative, and self-confidence. Those who have it prominent in their horoscope are able to put their ideals into practical action.

20-30° Sagittarius

The third decanate of Sagittarius is the Sagittarius-Leo or Jupiter-Jupiter-Sun-Sun decanate. Those with this decanate prominent in there horoscope possess great determination and optimism. Because of the Sun influence they often achieve positions of power and influence in educational, religious, or cultural institutions. They express their philosophic beliefs with power and authority, and are often able to inspire confidence and renewed faith in others. Very often these natives become prominent lawyers or judges, expressing the authority of Leo through the law, which is ruled by Jupiter. But there is also the danger of using religious and philosophic beliefs and institutional positions in a self-serving way, so these natives must be careful to avoid prejudice and biased viewpoints. They have a tendency, too, to become ego-identified with familiar and comfortable attitudes, even in the face of evidence to the contrary. Because of the fixed-sign nature of Leo these natives possess more determination and staying power than other Sagittarians. They should be careful not to become over optimistic, especially where speculation is concerned, but can go a long way down the road to success when they combine good judgment with their optimism.

Sagittarius Duads

0-2½° Sagittarius
The first duad of Sagittarius is the Sagittarius-Sagittarius or Jupiter-Jupiter-Jupiter-Jupiter duad. Because this duad is part of the Sagittarius decanate of Sagittarius, the qualities ascribed to the sign Sagittarius and the first decanate of Sagittarius apply to this duad in an intensified manner. Those with this duad prominent in the horoscope have a love of philosophy, higher education, travel, and sports. Because this is a mutable sign there is a triple mutable influence inherent in the duad, indicating great adaptability and flexibility of movement and action. These natives are able to draw upon many valuable lessons from the past and incorporate them into action. Their strong sense of history, combined with intuitive abilities associated with the triple-Jupiter influence gives these natives the capacity for prophetic insight into the future, especially if Jupiter or Neptune is located here.

2½-5° Sagittarius
The second duad of Sagittarius is the Sagittarius-Capricorn or Jupiter-Saturn duad. Those with this duad prominent in the horoscope are often attracted to legal, administrative, and political professions, and may become administrators in religious, governmental, educational, or charitable institutions. They generally hold conservative views on social, political, and religious matters, and are more cautious than the average Sagittarian. They are not apt to become unrealistic or over optimistic in their expansive endeavors since they have the ability to apply their visionary insight in a practical way. These natives are ambitious. They keep their own counsel and are often loners in the

pursuit of their goals; although this is not always apparent because they often work in the context of institutions and large organizations. There can be a great deal of travel for business and professional reasons.

5-7½° Sagittarius

The third duad of Sagittarius is the Sagittarius-Aquarius or Jupiter-Saturn-Uranus duad. This duad often produces visionary reformers and mystics of various types. These natives have a strong sense of future possibilities and ideal goals that could be achieved through social reform and the implementation of advanced ideas and scientific methods. There is an interest in improving the lot of others through the reform of existing religious, cultural, social, or political institutions. Because of Uranus they have strong prophetic and intuitive abilities, especially regarding the effects of new technological innovations influencing cultural evolution. These natives are fond of travel for adventure and experience, and usually have many friends associated with religious, cultural, or educational institutions, or among people from faraway places. Because of the Jupiter and Uranus influences they are able to befriend those less fortunate than themselves and extend a helping hand.

7½-10° Sagittarius

The fourth duad of Sagittarius is the Sagittarius-Pisces or Jupiter-Neptune duad. Because this duad is part of the Sagittarius decanate of Sagittarius, there is a triple (sign, decanate, and duad) Jupiter influence. Those with this duad prominent in the horoscope have strong visionary, mystical, religious tendencies and their creative, imaginative, and intuitive faculties are highly developed—especially if Jupiter or Neptune is found in this duad. There can be the capacity to foresee future events or have a feeling for what is happening in distant places. These natives often become associated with religious retreats, hospitals, or educational institutions. They are strong upholders of religious values and in some cases become prophets or leaders of religious cults. There can be strong fluctuations of mood and temperament caused by the combined combination of Sagittarius fire and Pisces water, sometimes causing alternating aggressiveness and possessiveness, which can be confusing and disturbing to others and may lead the native to confusion, muddle, and unrealistic optimism. If Jupiter or Neptune is found in this duad the qualities ascribed to it will be very evident.

10-12½° Sagittarius

The fifth duad of Sagittarius is the Sagittarius-Aries or Jupiter-Mars duad. Because this duad is part of the Aries decanate of Sagittarius, the qualities ascribed to the second decanate of Sagittarius apply to this duad in an intensified manner. Those with this duad prominent in the horoscope are strong, aggressive crusaders for their personal, social, religious, cultural, and educational beliefs, and have the motivation to apply those beliefs in the course of daily living. They seek to refine and improve existing conditions in these areas, and can spearhead religious and social reforms to help overcome corruption, indifference and lethargy. Because of the combined influences, advanced natives have deep insights into the causes of existing social issues and the actions needed to remedy those conditions. However, the average native is in danger of holding narrow-minded, aggressive, sectarian views. The result may be a competitive religious atmosphere that belies the basic principle of religious unity based on one spiritual reality. These natives are fond of travel to seek new adventures and experiences.

12½-15° Sagittarius

The sixth duad of Sagittarius is the Sagittarius-Taurus or Jupiter-Venus duad. Those with this duad prominent often have an interest in religious art and music, including such fields such as artistic and musical history, and the art forms of other cultures. Their strong interest in predicting business and financial trends often gives them an ability for stock market analysis and prediction. They can be attracted to the import-export business or businesses related to travel or education. These natives usually have utilitarian and conservative views on religious, philosophical, and cultural matters. A religion or philosophy is of no use to them unless it can be applied in a practical way and produces concrete results. An ability to foresee future trends often gives them unusual skills in money-making endeavors.

15-17½° Sagittarius

The seventh duad of Sagittarius is the Sagittarius-Gemini or Jupiter-Mercury duad. This duad often produces philosophic and religious writers, teachers, and lecturers. Those with this duad prominent in the horoscope are often attracted to work in the publishing industry or businesses related to travel and communication. Often they become teachers or researchers in universities or other cultural and educational institutions. Because this duad is part of the Aries decanate, these natives can be aggressive and forceful in promoting their ideas and theories and often compete to achieve a reputation for intellectual or scholarly distinction. Because Gemini and Sagittarius are mutable signs, these natives do not have the stamina or staying power of other Sagittarians; but they are adaptable and versatile. Their historical perspective and knowledge of many subjects can give them accurate insights into future events. These natives are full of plans for social improvement and for helping those in need, but they exist more in the mind than in practical action unless other factors in the horoscope balance this lack of practical application.

17½-20° Sagittarius

The eighth duad of Sagittarius is the Sagittarius-Cancer or Jupiter-Moon duad. These natives are highly intuitive and imaginative. They have a strong desire to incorporate religious values and cultural traditions into their home and family life, and have a strong sense of family loyalty. Their general attitudes are strongly influenced by their early family life, which may indicate a prejudiced outlook on life. They generally live far from their place of birth. Because this duad is part of the Aries decanate of Sagittarius, and because Aries and Cancer are cardinal signs, there can be a tendency to impulsive emotional behavior. Emotional extremes are indicated by the fire-water influences in this duad. The Jupiter emphasis can indicate overoptimism, especially among less advanced natives.

20-22½° Sagittarius

The ninth duad of Sagittarius is the Sagittarius-Leo or Jupiter-Sun duad. Because this duad is part of the Leo decanate of Sagittarius, the qualities ascribed to the third decanate of Sagittarius apply to this duad in an intensified manner. Those with this duad prominent in the horoscope seek distinction through cultural accomplishments or honors of some kind. Because of the double fixed-sign influence of the Leo decanate and duad, they have a great deal of staying power. Often there is a strong personal charisma that enables them to be influential in religious, educational, or cultural areas. Their self-confidence and strong belief in the causes they espouse inspires confidence in others. There is a lot of drama and pageantry incorporated into many of the activities they influence or take part in. They are apt to be authoritarian in their espousal and enforcement of their religious and ethical beliefs. Parades and elaborate religious ceremonies are typical of this kind of activity. They are fond of travel as a means of pursuing social and artistic interests.

22½-25° Sagittarius

The tenth duad of Sagittarius is the Sagittarius-Virgo or Jupiter-Mercury duad. These natives are inclined toward intellectual or scholarly pursuits, much as the seventh duad of this sign, but are more practical and meticulous in their orientation. They are often interested in spiritual healing and psychology as it affects the work and health of the general populace. Because Sagittarius and Virgo are both mutable signs, these natives are skillful in adapting to a variety of circumstances. The influence of the fixed Leo decanate gives them staying power. They can be farsighted in anticipating future needs and conditions related to work and industry, and thus make good industrial planners and trouble shooters.

25-27½° Sagittarius

The eleventh duad of Sagittarius is the Sagittarius-Libra or Jupiter-Venus duad. Because of the combination of Sagittarius overview and foresight and the self-confidence associated with the Leo decanate and the diplomacy of Libra, these natives have the ability to make good promoters and public relations people. Their exaltation of Saturn in Libra, combined with the Jupiter concern for law, often draws these natives into the legal profession. The Leo influence can make them convincing and forceful attorneys. The Leo-Libra combination can give an interest in religious forms of art and music or the cultural history of art forms. Those with this duad prominent are often associated with universities in these pursuits.

27½-30° Sagittarius

The twelfth duad of Sagittarius is the Sagittarius-Scorpio or Jupiter-Pluto-Mars duad. Those with this duad prominent in the horoscope are generally concerned with the reform and improvement of religious, cultural, educational, and legal institutions, often playing the role of muckraker in exposing corruption and inefficiency in these areas. These natives frequently act as promoters of corporate financial enterprises, or work with the business affairs of an institution in some way. They can be ruthless in defense of their principles, and may display a rigidity and fanaticism that endangers the very principles they are trying to defend.

Capricorn

Capricorn

Sign: Capricorn **Ruler:** Saturn

Capricorn Decanate 1: 0-10° Capricorn Ruler: Saturn

Capricorn Decanate 1 Duads:

0-2½° Capricorn	2½-5° Aquarius	5-7½° Pisces	7½-10° Aries
Ruler: Saturn	Rulers: Saturn, Uranus	Rulers: Jupiter, Neptune	Ruler: Mars

Capricorn Decanate 2: 10-20° Taurus Ruler: Venus

Capricorn Decanate 2 Duads:

10-12½° Taurus	12½-15° Gemini	15-17½° Cancer	17½-20° Leo
Ruler: Venus	Ruler: Mercury	Ruler: Moon	Ruler: Sun

Capricorn Decanate 3: 20-30° Virgo Ruler: Mercury

Capricorn Decanate 3 Duads:

20-22½° Virgo	22½-25° Libra	25-27½° Scorpio	27½-30° Sagittarius
Ruler: Mercury	Ruler: Venus	Rulers: Mars, Pluto	Ruler: Jupiter

Capricorn

The sign Capricorn falls in the earth triplicity. Hence, individuals with this sign prominent, like those of Taurus and Virgo, are motivated by practical considerations. But, unlike the natives of the other earth signs, individuals of the Capricorn disposition, by virtue of Capricorn's nature as a cardinal sign, achieve their practical objectives through constant activity. They possess an immediate practical awareness of their physical surroundings and little of practical consequence escapes their notice. Their deliberate and calculated modes of activity are augmented by their ability to make advantageous use of each opportunity for practical advancement.

Capricorn is a negative-feminine sign. Thus, natives of this temperament are not inclined to initiate actions on their own, but prefer to wait for situations that can be turned to their advantage by timely intervention.

Capricorn is ruled by Saturn, conferring those of its disposition with the capacity for patient, disciplined, and organized work They are strongly motivated by a desire for material status, respect in the eyes of the world, and financial independence, and they require practical managerial responsibilities to fulfill themselves.

It should be remembered that Mars, the desire and action planet, is exalted in Capricorn. Thus, although their actions may not be as forceful as those of Aries or Scorpio, they coordinate their activities within an organized strategy and are frequently more effective in the long run.

These individuals often live a longer than average life span and, subconsciously knowing this, seek security and independence for their old age.

Capricorn Decanates

0-10° Capricorn

The first decanate is the Capricorn-Capricorn or Saturn-Saturn decanate. Those with this decanate prominent are ambitious with good organizational and administrative ability, political astuteness, and the know-how to make most advantageous use of the opportunities offered. Because Mars is exalted in Capricorn, they act swiftly, forcefully, and decisively once they have determined the strategic time is at hand.

These natives are attracted to professions that will confer status, prestige, and security, so they can be looked up to and respected by the community. They are always aware of their present environment and how to make the most advantageous use of the opportunities it offers because Capricorn is a cardinal sign and this is a cardinal decanate. These natives will work long and hard to achieve their ends, and they are not afraid of the discipline and perseverance required to achieve a goal.

10-20° Capricorn

The second decanate of Capricorn is the Capricorn-Taurus or Saturn-Venus decanate. Those with this decanate prominent seek status and security through wealth, and may seek wealth through holding a high professional position or via a partnership or marriage. They often become executors and administrators in large-scale enterprises or manage their own business affairs. They make excellent accountants, financial analysts, and business trouble shooters.

Because Taurus is a fixed sign, these natives have tremendous staying power and perseverance to follow their endeavors through to a successful conclusion. There is a strong sense of value and a desire to own property of quality and enduring worth, but they should avoid the pitfall of worshiping money and material status as an end in itself. If they become too materialistic the emotional and spiritual values of life get lost. Then instead of owning possessions, they are enslaved by them.

20-30° Capricorn

The third decanate of Capricorn is the Capricorn-Virgo or Saturn-Mercury decanate. Those with this decanate prominent in the horoscope often are attracted to the medical profession and other fields where specialized skills and education confer status, financial advantage, and prestige. They have a talent for organizing and managing industrial production, making good trouble shooters, efficiency experts, and production managers. Because of the Saturn-Mercury combination they may be skilled in mathematics and attracted to such careers as engineering. Frequently they are absorbed into government clerical work as part of the machinery of some bureaucratic organization.

These Capricorns are more clothes-conscious than the other decanates of this sign. They like simplicity and elegance as a means of creating a good impression to further their business and career interests. They are inclined toward strict health and dietary regimens to improve their vitality, fitness, and appearance. These natives are particularly concerned with having good procedures and efficiency in their areas of work.

Capricorn Duads

0-2½° Capricorn
The first duad of Capricorn is the Capricorn-Capricorn or Saturn-Saturn duad. Because this duad is part of the Capricorn-Saturn decanate of Capricorn, the qualities ascribed to the sign Capricorn and the first decanate of Capricorn apply to this duad in an intensified manner. Those with this duad prominent are austere, hard-working, career-oriented, and perhaps almost too conservative. They are often attracted to legal, political, or business professions. Many natives of this duad become part of a government bureaucracy as clerks, administrators, or law enforcement personnel. They are methodical, organized, and purposeful in their method of achieving their ambitions. Older, well-established people often play an important part in helping them achieve success or the realization of their ambitions. As a result, even when young in years these natives become identified with the values of the older generation. Their sense of values is based on the practical usefulness of whatever they are dealing with. Things that cannot achieve concrete gains are of little interest or concern to them. These natives must avoid the danger of becoming crystallized and materialistic in their outlook.

2½-5° Capricorn
The second duad of Capricorn is the Capricorn-Aquarius or Saturn-Saturn-Uranus duad. Because this duad is part of the Capricorn decanate of Capricorn, there is a triple-Saturn influence that gives these natives well-organized minds and the ability needed for systematic scientific methodology. There can also be a strong interest in mathematics and the physical sciences. Those with this duad prominent in the horo-

scope have this sign's usual ambition and practicality, but are also receptive to new ideas and advanced methods of achieving their objectives, having the ability to use intuitive insight and original creative thinking to come up with solutions to administrative and professional problems. They are intellectual, and less bound up in tradition than the average Capricorn. These natives often have a strong interest in professional groups and organizations, where they work effectively in groups and teams and will cooperate with others to achieve worthwhile goals.

5-7½° Capricorn

The third duad of Capricorn is the Capricorn-Pisces or Saturn-Jupiter-Neptune duad. Those with this duad prominent in the horoscope can further their ambitions through the use of creative imagination and insight. They love secrecy and behind-the-scenes planning. Often more intuitive, visionary, expansive, and sensitive to aesthetics than the average Capricorn, they are able to pick up subtle clues and nuances and build them into skillful strategies to achieve their ambitions. There is the danger of being prey to subconscious fears and neuroses that result in an irrational need for material security at any cost. Often they are concerned with the preservation of their reputations. These natives can become administrators or organizers in religious, educational, governmental, or cultural institutions.

7½-10° Capricorn

The fourth duad of Capricorn is the Capricorn-Aries or Saturn-Mars duad. Since this duad has a triple cardinal-sign influence and a triple-Mars influence, these natives are very aggressive and competitive in pursuing their professional ambitions and achieving their desires. They do not always have the same patience over the long haul as other Capricorns, although when they work they work hard. They are seldom lazy, and never lack initiative. Those with this duad prominent have very little patience with weakness or laziness in others. They pride themselves on being strong and able to cope with any situation. Many of them are attracted to military careers. They make aggressive and hard-working entrepreneurs and industrialists. Their weakness is a tendency to be self-centered in their ambitions and to ignore the rights and feelings of others. They have a special ability to act with courage and decisiveness in emergency situations, and to take advantage of opportunities.

10-12½° Capricorn

The fifth duad of Capricorn is the Capricorn-Taurus or Saturn-Venus duad. Because this duad is part of the Taurus decanate of Capricorn, the qualities ascribed to the second decanate of Capricorn apply to this duad in an intensified manner. Because of the triple earth-sign influence, these natives can be sensuous and attracted to creature comforts and the good things of the earth. The double-Venus influence gives a strong sense of beauty and refinement. Their aesthetic tastes are along traditional lines because of the Venus-Saturn combination. These natives seek possessions of beauty and quality to enhance their status and security. Those with this duad prominent in the horoscope are deliberate and cautious in making decisions, but once they have chosen a course of action are not easily deterred. They are oriented toward business and commerce and often become executives or business managers. These natives should be careful that they do not become so materialistic as to negate human values and the emotional well-being of others. If they forget that things are for people and that people should not be used for things, unhappiness and failure is the probable result.

12½-15° Capricorn

The sixth duad of Capricorn is the Capricorn-Gemini or Saturn-Mercury duad. Those with this duad prominent have well-organized intellectual abilities. Their professional responsibilities often involve writing, communication, travel, lecturing, and teaching, and they often have talent in mathematics, physical sciences, or other areas requiring logic and disciplined thinking. These natives have the ability to arrive at original, practical solutions to professional problems, and use knowledge and education as a means for career advancement and recognition. They instinctively know that the more knowledgeable they are concerning their work the faster they will advance in it. Because this duad belongs to a cardinal sign, a fixed decanate, and itself has a mutable influence, these natives have a good blend of adaptability, decisiveness, and perseverance. Since Gemini is an air sign, they are more intellectual than the average Capricorn, who is concerned primarily with material values.

15-17½° Capricorn

The seventh duad of Capricorn is the Capricorn-Cancer or Saturn-Moon duad. Those with this duad prominent in the horoscope have a strong sense of family pride. The profession they choose and matters concerning their profession are often influenced by their family conditioning or upbringing. They seldom travel except for business reasons, and often live in one place for many years. Since they have a strong need for stability and security in the home, they seek marriages and professional and domestic situations that confer social status and domestic security. They have strong family and domestic instincts because the Moon is exalted in Taurus (the decanate to which this duad belongs) and also rules Cancer. If the Moon is located here these qualities will be greatly emphasized. The social, political, and ethical values of these natives are usually conservative, and would be considered by many to be old-fashioned. Because of the Saturn-Moon combination they tend to be shy, emotionally reserved, and formal in their personal mannerisms. That Saturn-Moon combination also means they must guard against emotional depression. The professional and business affairs of these natives are often related to farming, the selling and distribution of foodstuffs, or are related in some way to women or the public.

17½-20° Capricorn

The eighth duad of Capricorn is the Capricorn-Leo or Saturn-Sun duad. There is a double fixed-sign influence in this duad from the Taurus decanate and Leo duad, so those with this duad prominent pursue their ambitions with great determination, intensity, and perseverance. This combination gives artistic ability and a flair for the dramatic along with an excellent sense of composition and structure. These natives have a strong leadership ability because of the managerial skills of Capricorn combined with the personal charisma of Leo. They have a tendency to become involved in speculative financial endeavors, often including the entertainment industry. Many market analysts and investment managers are apt to have this duad prominent in the horoscope. There is great personal pride associated with this duad, and a need to be in the spotlight or to receive personal recognition.

20-22½° Capricorn

The ninth duad of Capricorn is the Capricorn-Virgo or Saturn-Mercury duad. Because this duad is part of the Virgo decanate of Capricorn, the qualities ascribed to the third decanate of Capricorn apply to this duad in an intensified manner. Those with this duad prominent in the horoscope are endowed with practical intelligence, especially in their work and professional affairs, and particularly if Mercury or Saturn is located here. They are often attracted to medical or highly skilled technological professions, and have a talent for such fields as accounting and the physical sciences because of the mathematical ability conferred by the Mercury-Saturn combination. They are well organized and precise, efficient, and methodical in their work. These natives are conservative and meticulous in dress and hygiene. They associate the manner of dress and deportment with status and making a good impression for professional and business reasons.

22½-25° Capricorn

The tenth duad of Capricorn is the Capricorn-Libra or Saturn-Venus duad. Because Saturn is exalted in Libra and rules Capricorn there is a double-Saturn influence inherent in this duad that gives these natives a strong sense of justice, social propriety, and protocol that enables them to be successful in such fields as diplomacy, public relations, law, and politics. Those with this duad prominent have a good memory for detail in legal affairs and interpersonal relationships because this duad is part of the Virgo decanate of Capricorn. They are more intellectual and communicative than the average Capricorn as a result of the air-sign influence of Libra and Mercury's influence in the Virgo decanate. Because of the Venus influence these natives are also less shy and reserved. The cardinal-sign qualities associated with this duad mean these natives are able to take skillful advantage of the moment. As with the previous duad there is a strong sense of personal deportment, but with more emphasis on artistic creativity in personal dress.

25-27½° Capricorn
The eleventh duad of Capricorn is the Capricorn-Scorpio or Saturn-Mars-Pluto duad. Those with this duad prominent in the horoscope often are involved in industry and corporate business. Because of the Mars-Saturn combination they tend to be stern and Spartan with little tolerance for weakness or laziness in others since they despise it in themselves. This makes them hard, exacting taskmasters, often attracted to military careers. They have great expertise and resourcefulness in their work. Their determined, hardworking nature often leads to positions of leadership and authority if they do not become so ruthless that they alienate others.

27½-30° Capricorn
The twelfth duad of Capricorn is the Capricorn-Sagittarius or Saturn-Jupiter duad. Because this duad is part of the Virgo decanate, there is a double mutable sign influence that indicates adaptability. Those with this duad prominent often become administrators in educational, religious, government, and medical institutions. They have prophetic vision and insight into legal, political, cultural, and sociological changes. These natives may be attracted to a legal or political career as a result of Jupiter's concern with the law. They have strong ethical and moral values along traditional lines, and often desire to apply the principles of philosophy to professional affairs. They usually deal justly with others in their professional and business endeavors.

Aquarius

Aquarius

Sign: Aquarius   **Ruler:** Uranus, Saturn

Aquarius Decanate 1: 0-10° Aquarius   Ruler: Uranus, Saturn

Aquarius Decanate 1 Duads:

0-2½° Aquarius	2½-5° Pisces	5-7½° Aries	7½-10° Taurus
Ruler: Uranus, Saturn	Ruler Neptune, Jupiter	Ruler Mars	Ruler Venus

Aquarius Decanate 2: 10-20° Gemini   Ruler: Mercury

Aquarius Decanate 2 Duads:

10-12½° Gemini	12½-15° Cancer	15-17½° Leo	17½-20° Virgo
Ruler: Mercury	Ruler: Moon	Ruler: Sun	Ruler: Mercury

Aquarius Decanate 3: 20-30° Libra   Ruler: Venus

Aquarius Decanate 3 Duads:

20-22½° Libra	22½-25° Scorpio	25-27½° Sagittarius	27½-30° Capricorn
Ruler: Venus	Rulers: Pluto, Mars	Ruler: Jupiter	Ruler: Saturn

Aquarius

Aquarius falls in the air triplicity. Hence, those with this sign prominent are intellectually-oriented and concerned with ideas of universal humanitarian or scientific implication. Likewise, Aquarius' nature as a fixed sign inclines those of its bent to pursue mental goals with steady purpose unlike the vacillations of Gemini and the scale-tipping of Libra. They will not accept any idea or standard of conduct on faith alone. They respect only those ideas and principles that can be proven scientifically or through direct experience. And, they will not adhere to authority they cannot respect. This is why this sign is so closely associated with reformers and revolutionaries. However, when natives of the Aquarian temperament do change their minds, frequent or infrequent as it may be, they do so abruptly and unexpectedly, to the point of confusing and shocking others.

Aquarius' nature as a positive-masculine sign inclines individuals of its temperament to take the initiative in formulating and implementing new ideas and practices. Mercury's exaltation here confers highly-developed intellectual abilities which, when combined with the intuitive inspiration and original ideas provided by Uranus' natural rulership, imparts to those of the Aquarian disposition the ability to research important scientific discoveries and to invent and innovate new techniques, theories and methodologies.

The objective view of reality assumed by those with Aquarius prominent evokes an innate interest in large-scale social and humanitarian unfoldment, and because of their impartiality of viewpoint they are apt to acquire a great many friends and are frequently associated with scientific, political, and humanitarian groups.

Aquarius Decanates

0-10° Aquarius

The first decanate of Aquarius is the Aquarius-Aquarius or Uranus-Saturn-Uranus-Saturn decanate. Those with this decanate prominent in the horoscope often seek new experiences as a means of expanding their knowledge and intellectual outlook. Their strong desire to break away from tradition and try new ways of doing things often takes the form of rebellion against the materialistic values that cause people to be used as a means of gaining possessions and status.

These natives have a strong interest in scientifically understanding basic laws of nature—not only scientific laws but the spiritual laws of human destiny and evolution as well. They have a broad and impartial outlook that gives no special advantages or disadvantages to anyone unless they have been earned. It should be remembered that Saturn (which co-rules Aquarius) is exalted in Libra, the sign of justice.

Because of the double fixed-sign influence of this decanate these natives adhere to what they consider to be right and will not permit their minds to be changed against their will. They are friendly and cooperative on a voluntary basis, but will not submit to regimentation or blind authority in any form. They are capable of mental concentration, which can bring them intuitive guidance.

10-20° Aquarius

The second decanate of Aquarius is the Aquarius-Gemini or Uranus-Saturn-Mercury decanate. Because Mercury is exalted in Aquarius and rules Gemini, there is a double-Mercury influence that makes these natives intellectual and fond of discussion and communication with friends and associates. The Mercury-Uranus combination indicates a quick, intuitive, original mind. They often have unusual ability in scientific and occult studies. Many inventors have this decanate prominent in the horoscope.

Because Gemini is a mutable sign, these natives are more adaptable than other Aquarians. They have intense curiosity and a desire to know the underlying causes behind things of interest to them that may lead to surprising and original solutions to problems. They acquire much knowledge through friendships and group associations, often resulting in travel.

20-30° Aquarius

The third decanate of Aquarius is the Aquarius-Libra or Saturn-Uranus-Venus decanate. Saturn is co-ruler of Aquarius and exalted in Libra, giving this decanate a double-Saturn influence so that these natives have a strong sense of purpose and responsibility in achieving worthwhile scientific, social, humanitarian, or organizational goals.

There is a strong interest in such fields as psychology, sociology, and human relations. These natives often become leaders and organizers of group endeavors. They are friendly and sociable, but seem formal and austere in their social behavior. Extremely loyal in friendship, they expect loyalty and responsibility in return. They have a strong ambition to achieve intellectual and social distinction in some way.

Aquarius Duads

0-2½° Aquarius

The first duad of Aquarius is the Aquarius-Aquarius or Uranus-Saturn-Uranus-Saturn duad. Because this duad is part of the Aquarius decanate of Aquarius, the qualities ascribed to the sign Aquarius and the first decanate of Aquarius apply to this duad in an intensified manner. These natives have a great faculty for original thought and for finding new and scientific ways of doing things. Their strong desire to break away from traditions and routines that no longer serve a useful purpose often leads them to become social reformers and innovators. Because of the triple fixed-sign emphasis of this duad, they adhere to their own point of view when they have strong convictions about something. They can also change their minds drastically and unexpectedly, but they can never be coerced into doing so. These natives prefer to work in association with others rather than by themselves. Their strong tendency to seek new experiences as a means of breaking out of mentally limiting routines and old conditions makes for a strong love of excitement and adventure, especially in the realm of the mind.

2½-5° Aquarius

The second duad of Aquarius is the Aquarius-Pisces or Uranus-Saturn-Jupiter-Neptune duad. Because of the Uranus-Neptune combination, these natives often have an unusual intuitive and clairvoyant ability. They can know things without understanding why they know them, and often see further into the future than the logical mind normally can. A strong intuitive understanding of the thoughts and feelings of others can be expanded to the level of penetrating insights into social conditions and trends. Those with this duad prominent often have a strong humanitarian desire to help the underdog. This idealistic tendency can produce much good if it is directed with wisdom and practicality. Because of the Uranus-Neptune combination and Saturn's co-rulership of Aquarius and the Aquarius decanate, these natives have the ability to express their original ideas and creative imagination in an organized and practical way.

5-7½° Aquarius
The third duad of Aquarius is the Aquarius-Aries or Uranus-Saturn-Mars duad. Those with this duad prominent are often the typical revolutionary Aquarian and can be militant promoters of social change. Because of the Mars-Uranus combination there is a tendency to be impatient and demand action now. They seek excitement and adventure through new experiences, but because Aquarius is a fixed-sign and co-ruled by Saturn, they are able to follow through once they start something. These natives can exercise good judgment and do organized planning if they are willing to make the effort. As long as what they are doing is of interest to them they work hard and energetically, but when the job becomes boring, monotonous, and routine they turn restless and seek change. Because of the Saturn-Mars-Uranus combination they have good mechanical, electronic, or engineering abilities, especially if Uranus or Saturn is located here. The Mars-Uranus combination indicates the danger of explosive anger, especially when it is pent up by the Saturn influence. Without being recognized or dealt with in a conscious manner, transit Mars will often set off a tirade when making adverse aspects to a placement in this duad.

7½-10° Aquarius
The fourth duad of Aquarius is the Aquarius-Taurus or Uranus-Saturn-Venus duad. These natives often become involved in the promotion of technological inventions and innovations. Because of the triple fixed-sign emphasis inherent in this duad they are capable of an immovable determination when dedicated to a goal or ideal. Those with this duad prominent often have pleasing, harmonious and friendly personal mannerisms except when annoyed or opposed. They can have unorthodox ideas concerning marriage, romance, and sexual mores because of the Venus-Uranus combination, and often there is an eccentric sense of values regarding money and personal possessions. This combination of Uranus and Venus could also indicate an unusual artistic flair or talent.

10-12½° Aquarius
The fifth duad of Aquarius is the Aquarius-Gemini or Uranus-Saturn-Mercury duad. Because this duad is part of the Gemini decanate of Aquarius, the qualities ascribed to the second decanate of Aquarius apply to this duad in an intensified manner. These na-

tives have a triple-Mercury influence because Mercury is exalted in Aquarius and rules the Gemini decanate and duad. The triple air-sign emphasis of this duad makes the natives emotionally detached and aloof, although friendly and communicative in an intellectual way. They are more adaptable and less fixed than other Aquarians because of the mutable influence here. Those with this duad prominent in the horoscope have brilliant, intuitive minds because of the Uranus-Mercury combination and solve problems by tapping a superconscious level of intelligence. There is the ability to understand, and possibly the ability to write about profound occult and scientific ideas. These natives often have a strong interest in electronic media and technological skill in this area. They do much communication with friends and associates, and because of their advanced intellectual capacity are often influential through their ideas. There is much traveling or coming and going because of friendships, associations, organizational endeavors, and intellectual and scientific pursuits.

12½-15° Aquarius

The sixth duad of Aquarius is the Aquarius-Cancer or Uranus-Saturn-Moon duad. Those with this duad prominent often include their friends as family members. Much group intellectual or scientific activity goes on in the home. Natives are interested in modern improvements for the home and new approaches to family life. They are less aloof and detached than other Aquarians because Cancer is an emotional water sign, which gives them emotional empathy and sympathy. Because Aquarius is a fixed-sign, Gemini is mutable, and Cancer is cardinal, these natives have the capacity to use determination, adaptability, and decisive action in a well-integrated synthesis.

15-17½° Aquarius

The seventh duad of Aquarius is the Aquarius-Leo or Uranus-Saturn-Sun duad. Aquarius and Leo are fixed signs; consequently, natives with this duad prominent have strong willpower and the ability to follow through with endeavors. Because this duad is part of the Gemini decanate of Aquarius, they have the ability and skill to choose from a variety of methods to achieve their goals. Natives of this duad are independent, and they resent interference on the part of others. They have the ability to assume a leadership role among friends, groups, or organizations.

17½-20° Aquarius

The eighth duad of Aquarius is the Aquarius-Virgo or Uranus-:Saturn-Mercury duad. Since it is part of the Gemini decanate of Aquarius, and Mercury is exalted in Aquarius, there is a triple-Mercury influence indicating a high degree of intelligence and practical ability—even more so if Mercury is found here. Because of the Mercury-Uranus combination, these natives are often skilled in electronic, technological and medical fields. There may be an interest in advanced healing techniques, diet, and the use of subtle electronic or occult forces in healing. Since Virgo is an earth sign, those with this duad prominent in the horoscope will apply their intellectual abilities in a practical way. There will be much communication and coming and going in connection with work and intellectual concerns. There is also a fondness for unique and attractive wearing apparel.

20-22½° Aquarius

The ninth duad of Aquarius is the Aquarius-Libra or Uranus-Saturn-Venus duad. Because this duad is part of the Libra decanate of Aquarius, the qualities ascribed to the third decanate of Aquarius apply to this duad in an intensified manner. Saturn's exaltation in the Libra decanate and duad, combined with Saturn's co-rulership of Aquarius, gives a triple-Saturn influence that gives these natives excellent ability in mental organization and the coordination of group, organizational, and political activities. They have a strong sense of loyalty to friends and coworkers, but expect fair treatment in return. These natives are very good at public relations, especially as it applies to groups and organizations, and they are greatly interested in psychology and what motivates people. There can be original talent in artistic composition because of the double-Venus, Saturn, and Uranus influences.

22½-25° Aquarius

The tenth duad of Aquarius is the Aquarius-Scorpio or Aries-Uranus-Saturn-Pluto-Mars duad. Because Uranus rules Aquarius and is exalted in Scorpio, there is a double-Uranus influence inherent in this duad. According to the writings of Alice Bailey, Uranus is the esoteric ruler of Libra, which would give a further Uranus emphasis to this duad through the Libra decanate to which it belongs. This strong Uranus influence indicates strong intuitive abilities, occult interests, and the resourceful use of modern technology. In advanced individuals the will can be used to control and direct occult energies. Often there is skill in handling the technological and corporate business affairs associated with engineering projects and large-scale research and development. Because Scorpio and Aquarius are both fixed signs these natives can be relentless in the pursuit of their goals and achieving their ambitions. They are capable of decisive action and have the necessary determination to finish what they start. They are very resourceful, and able to intuitively arrive at solutions to problems that seem insurmountable to others.

25-27½° Aquarius

The eleventh duad of Aquarius is the Aquarius-Sagittarius or Uranus-Saturn-Jupiter duad. Because of the Uranus-Jupiter combination in this duad these natives can be highly intuitive and prophetic. They have a strong interest in social, cultural, and religious reform because they can see what will happen if the necessary changes are not made. There is also an interest in new and innovative educational techniques and a strong leaning toward occult philosophy and religion. They often make good writers, teachers, and lecturers because of Mercury's exaltation in Aquarius and Jupiter's influence in Sagittarius. There is a combined fixed, cardinal, and mutable influence in this duad that enables these natives to initiate action, adapt to changing circumstances, and to follow through to the end of an endeavor. Interesting and unexpected things happen to them while traveling or pursuing higher knowledge.

27½-30° Aquarius

The twelfth duad of Aquarius is the Aquarius-Capricorn or Uranus-Saturn-Saturn duad. These natives have a triple-Saturn influence (Saturn rules Capricorn, is exalted in Libra, and co-rules Aquarius) that gives them a strong sense of personal discipline and responsibility, good organization, and managerial ability. They often become administrators in technical research or engineering fields. Their outlook on life is serious, and sometimes their personal mannerisms are austere, especially if Saturn is found in this duad. The Saturn influence also confers mathematical ability to many who have this duad prominent. Because Libra and Capricorn are both cardinal signs these natives are capable of decisive action and usually keep themselves busy. They seek to turn their intellectual abilities to practical benefit because of the earth-sign nature of Capricorn. They are highly conscious of their surroundings and well informed concerning what goes on in the world. There is a strong interest in political and business reform and improvement.

Pisces

Pisces

Sign: Pisces **Ruler:** Jupiter, Neptune

Pisces Decanate 1: 0-10° Pisces   Rulers: Jupiter, Neptune

Pisces Decanate 1 Duads:

0-2½° Pisces	2½-5° Aries	5-7½° Taurus	7½-10° Gemini
Rulers: Jupiter, Neptune	Ruler: Mars	Ruler: Venus	Ruler: Mercury

Pisces Decanate 2: 10-20° Cancer   Ruler: Moon

Pisces Decanate 2 Duads:

10-12½° Cancer	12½-15° Leo	15-17½° Virgo	17½-20° Libra
Ruler: Moon	Ruler: Sun	Ruler: Mercury	Ruler: Venus

Pisces Decanate 3: 20-30° Scorpio   Ruler: Mars, Pluto

Pisces Decanate 3 Duads:

20-22½° Scorpio	22½-25° Sagittarius	25-27½° Capricorn	27½-30° Aquarius
Ruler: Mars, Pluto	Ruler: Jupiter	Ruler: Saturn	Rulers: Uranus, Saturn

Pisces

The sign Pisces falls in the water triplicity. Hence, individuals of this temperament are largely motivated by feelings, emotions and intuition. Likewise, Pisces' nature as a mutable sign inclines those of its bent to draw upon past experience retained in the subconscious memory to make decisions and formulate a way of life.

Pisces is probably the most introverted of all the signs, a quality becoming to its negative-feminine nature. Natives with this sign prominent are engaged in an internal process of assimilation and understanding of a whole cycle of past experience in preparation for a new beginning, expressed through the following sign, Aries.

Jupiter's and Neptune's co-rulership of this sign confers those of its disposition with strong religious feelings, usually based upon an internal intuitive perception of spiritual reality rather than upon external cultural conditioning, like those of Sagittarius.

These individuals are highly susceptible to subliminal influences and emotional nuances within their environment and, subconsciously aware of this, they seek a quiet, secluded setting for protection in the exercise of their sensitive psyches. For this reason, they are often found in large institutions or places of retreat that offer maximum personal anonymity.

Venus' exaltation in Pisces endows these individuals with an extreme sensitivity to beauty, and the Neptunian imagination, when combined with this Venusian influence, often results in artistic or musical ability. Beauty in music, art, or nature possesses a tremendous healing effect for those of Piscean temperament.

Pisces is generally considered to be the most psychic sign, and those with this sign prominent often manifest prophetic visions of the future, telepathic ability, or an acute awareness of the past.

Pisces Decanates

0-10° Pisces
The first decanate of Pisces is the Pisces-Pisces or Jupiter-Neptune-Jupiter-Neptune decanate. Because these natives tend to be introspective and meditative, there is an intuitive ability to understand the feelings of others as the result of an emotional telepathic link that exists between these natives and those around them.

Venus is exalted in Pisces, and Neptune confers imagination, visualization, and clairvoyant faculties, so those with this duad prominent often express themselves through art and music. Their ability to create moods and illusions can make them fine actors. These natives have a strong link with their subconscious mind and the subliminal impressions that flow from it, so they are easily influenced by the subtle nuances of their environment, which often subconsciously reminds them of past experiences. Their openness to impressions can make them feel ill at ease without consciously knowing why, but it also makes them more appreciative and aware of beauty.

Although this decanate helps its natives to tap the accumulated wisdom of their subconscious resources, there is the danger of neurotic or psychotic reactions no longer appropriate to the present situation if their subconscious memories are associated with pain and unpleasantness and are not properly understood.

These natives are often associated with hospitals or institutions, working behind the scenes. They are compassionate and sympathetic toward those less fortunate than themselves because of a subconscious remembrance of similar circumstances in their own past.

10-20° Pisces
The second decanate of Pisces is the Pisces-Cancer or Jupiter-Neptune-Moon decanate. Because Jupiter and Neptune are exalted in Cancer they have a double influence that is

similar to the influence of Jupiter and Neptune in the first decanate. These natives use the home as a place of spiritual retreat, contemplation, and imaginative artistic expression. Like Cancer's natives, those with this duad prominent in the horoscope have a tendency to want to mother the world, so their home is often used as a place to help those less fortunate.

These natives generally lavish much time and energy on the home, making it beautiful and artistically pleasing, because Pisces is an artistic sign. They can have a talent for gourmet cooking and, so to speak, "cook with love."

Since Cancer is a cardinal sign these natives can act decisively when they feel a pressing emotional need to do so. Often they have close psychic, karmic, and emotional links with other family members.

20-30° Pisces

The third decanate of Pisces is the Pisces-Scorpio or Jupiter-Neptune-Mars-Pluto decanate. This is one of the most occult decanates of the zodiac because of the combined influences of Uranus (exalted in Scorpio), Neptune (ruler of Pisces), and Pluto (ruler of Scorpio). These outer planets are all concerned with the evolution of man's higher intuitive and spiritual faculties.

Those with this decanate prominent in the horoscope have greater willpower, strength, and determination than the average Pisces, due to the Mars, Pluto, and Uranus, influence of Scorpio. There is apt to be more follow-through with projects they start, and great resourcefulness. They are able to use past experiences to improve existing circumstances and initiate new enterprises.

Because this is the last decanate of the zodiac it is intimately associated with the spiritual process of death and rebirth. The native is engaged in the job of regenerating and making the subconscious mind become conscious in preparation for the new cycle of evolutionary experiences beginning in Aries. Mars and Pluto, which co-rule the Scorpio decanate, indicate the complete Plutonian process of death in this decanate, and rebirth in the first decanate of Aries. All of the accumulated debris of the subconscious mind that no longer serves a useful purpose must be consumed by the transmuting fire of Pluto. This is one of the most powerful, intense, and interesting phases of the zodiacal cycle or spiral of evolutionary growth.

Needless to say, these natives have a great emotional intensity that they must learn to direct in a calm, centered way. Just as there is great calm and peace at the center of a hurricane, so these natives must find the center or "eye" of their own emotional storms. They can do so by developing their spiritual will or the faculty of awareness of self.

If the native has planets in this decanate, or if this decanate falls on one of the angular house cusps, affairs ruled by the planets can be brought into harmony through meditation and spiritual improvement. The native must be willing to accept fundamental change and spiritual growth in this area.

Many inspired geniuses, including Albert Einstein, who had the Sun located here, have had this decanate prominent in the horoscope. It often confers profound insights into the fundamental laws of the universe.

Pisces Duads

0-2½° Pisces

The first duad is the Pisces-Pisces or Jupiter-Neptune-Jupiter-Neptune duad. Because this duad is part of the Pisces decanate of Pisces, the qualities ascribed to Pisces and the first decanate of Pisces apply to this duad in an intensified manner. Those with this duad prominent are entering into the Piscean phase of introspective self-analysis. Their values and emotional reactions are strongly colored by past experiences, and because of their depth of experience there is a breadth of understanding and compassion for all people. They have highly developed imaginations and psychic visualization abilities, and are creative in many areas, especially the arts. Idle daydreaming should be avoided since they must work to apply their inspiration if they are to be effective. The triple mutable-sign emphasis of this duad makes these natives versatile and adaptable, but can result in emotional instability. They may also be prone to emotional extremes, from peaceful meditative states to distraught and impassioned tirades, because Neptune is a planet of extremes and gives a tendency to go overboard in things. Their sympathetic nature causes natives of this duad to be pulled easily into the emotional problems of others, so they must learn to detach themselves from the negative conditions of those they are helping. This does not mean to avoid helping others, but that one must remain calm and detached in order to provide real assistance. It is impossible to pull someone else out of the mud if you are stuck in it yourself. These natives wish to attempt large-scale endeavors but are not always practical or realistic in their expectations. They can have a peculiar type of luck that is really a karmic protection based on past good actions.

2½-5° Pisces

The second duad of Pisces is the Pisces-Aries or Jupiter-Neptune-Mars duad. Those with this duad prominent can have a peculiar and contradictory psychological makeup, at one moment aggressive and the next retiring. They can be competitive and self-assertive in subtle ways. Their desire to use intuitive faculties to gain personal authority in leadership is a reason for taking care that supposed spiritual guidance is not actually personal egotism or ambition for power. The religious inclination of Jupiter and Neptune often makes these natives aggressive crusaders for whatever religious cult or dogma they subscribe to. They often disguise personal egotism or sublimate it within the group egotism involved in whichever particular doctrine they uphold. Devotees of religious and mystical cults often make this mistake. On the positive side there may be the desire to actively help those in need and to improve the prevailing social order. They are often inspired to initiate worthwhile projects, and are more inclined than the average Pisces to put their inspiration into action.

5-7½° Pisces

The third duad of Pisces is the Pisces-Taurus or Jupiter-Neptune-Venus duad. Those with this duad prominent in the horoscope have a triple-Venus influence (sign, decanate, and duad). They excel in music and other creative, artistic expression because of their tremendous love of beauty and sensitivity to it. The earthy Taurus influence is combined with the imagination of Neptune to make them sensuous. These natives are more aware of the financial side of life than is the average Pisces because they wish to attract to themselves lovely things that require money. If these desires are unregulated there can also be compulsive spending. Since Taurus is a fixed sign these natives persevere and do not vacillate like other Pisces natives.

7½-10° Pisces

The fourth duad of Pisces is the Pisces-Gemini or Jupiter-Neptune-Mercury duad. Those with this duad prominent must avoid a tendency toward vacillation and indecisiveness indicated by the triple mutable-sign influence inherent in this duad. Since Gemini and Pisces square each other in the natural zodiac and their rulers—Mercury, Jupiter, and Neptune—also square each other through their rulership of Virgo and Sagittarius respectively, there is an important karmic lesson in the proper use of the mind and imagination to be learned from this duad. These natives possess great imagination and, often, intuitive telepathic ability. (Many psychic readers, and others who channel information from psychic realms, have this duad prominent.) There is also talent for inspirational writing, poetry, and other forms of creative literary expression. If these natives do not put their ideas into action their talents decline and others must put their ideas into use. They must also avoid dissipating their energy by scattering their attention on too many things at once. Because of their imaginative and intuitive approach these natives do not adapt well to ordinary academic disciplines and are often regarded as enigmas or problem students by their teachers. Discipline must come through their own inner guidance and is not easily imposed by external forces. They are easily distracted by subliminal environmental disturbances and subconscious mental or emotional processes, but once they are clear about their direction and purpose in life they are highly capable, and possess many insights into themselves.

10-12½° Pisces

The fifth duad is the Pisces-Cancer or Jupiter-Neptune-Moon duad. Because this duad is part of the Cancer decanate of Pisces, the qualities ascribed to the second decanate of Pisces apply to this duad in an intensified manner. Those with this duad prominent are very psychic and emotionally sensitive. In fact, their emotions are so strong these natives must be careful not to let them overpower their reason. Because of the highly developed powers of imagination and visualization inherent in this duad, many mediums and psychics are found here. These natives have great generosity, compassion, and sympathy for others, but it must be tempered with wisdom. Highly developed natives can be generous and magnanimous, helping those less fortunate than themselves. Some people with this duad prominent acquire great wealth and power by means of the Jupiter influence here. Many religious and cultural activities are carried on in the home, and there is a strong desire to incorporate religious values into family life. A strong maternal instinct is associated with this duad, especially among women natives.

12½-15° Pisces

The sixth duad of Pisces is the Pisces-Leo or Jupiter-Neptune-Sun duad. Those with this duad prominent in the horoscope have a strong sense of the dramatic. They are often actors or performing artists, or have a tendency in that direction. They may also have a flair for painting or dramatic music. Their natural love and empathy for children can make them very emotional, and they can become very intense and emotional over their own romantic affairs. These natives can alternate in an unexpected manner between aggressive self-confidence and a shy, retiring manner. Because Leo is a fixed sign they are apt to be more determined and to have more staying power than the average Pisces, and can be incessant in their subtle attempts to get what they want despite a tendency toward indolence and procrastination. In some cases there is an inclination to speculate or gamble, which is often based on hunches or inner feelings.

15-17½° Pisces

The seventh duad of Pisces is the Pisces-Virgo or Jupiter-Neptune-Mercury duad. These natives often make excellent gourmet cooks because of the Virgo and Cancer influence. Their work can be involved with nursing, medicine, hospitals, psychiatric institutions, or spiritual healing or diet. Advanced natives of this duad are able to diagnose illness by using their intuitive or clairvoyant faculties. Because of the Mercury-Neptune combination, their work is often secret in some way. Those with this duad prominent in the horoscope have nervous systems that are highly sensitive so they must avoid strain and maintain an attitude of detachment in order not to take on the emotional conditions and illnesses of others. They are fond of attractive, artistic modes of dress. Women of this duad often wear exotic perfume or jewelry and other personal adornments.

17½-20° Pisces

The eighth duad of Pisces is the Pisces-Libra or Jupiter-Neptune-Venus duad. These natives often display exceptional musical and artistic talent since Pisces and Libra are both artistic signs, and especially if Venus is found here. Venus is exalted in Pisces and rules Libra, thus having a double-influence and providing a strong sense of beauty and refinement to those who have this duad prominent. The Venus-Neptune combination adds inspired imagination and creative insight. Many composers are natives of this duad. Because this duad is part of the Cancer decanate, its creative talent is often employed in beautifying the home. Saturn's exaltation in Libra gives a good sense of structural composition and mastery of technique. The Libra-Pisces-Venus-Neptune combination can give an ability or interest in psychology. The double cardinal-sign influence here makes these natives socially outgoing, more so than the average shy, retiring Pisces. They have a tendency to avoid rough conditions, uncouth people, and coarse surroundings. Disharmony in the environment makes them ill at ease, even physically ill.

20-22½° Pisces

The ninth duad of Pisces is the Pisces-Scorpio or Jupiter-Neptune-Mars-Pluto duad. Because this duad is part of the Scorpio decanate of Pisces, the qualities ascribed to the third decanate of Pisces apply to this duad in an intensified manner. Those with this duad prominent have unusual psychic and occult abilities because of the influence of all three outer planets—Neptune (rules Pisces), Pluto (rules the Scorpio duad and decanate), and Uranus (exalted in this duad and decanate). There can be a strong interest in advanced scientific fields, parapsychology, metaphysics, and reincarnation. Because of the strong Scorpio influence these natives have greater strength and determination than the average Pisces. They are compassionate but have little tolerance for weakness or laziness. They are often associated with secretive work of some kind, or things that go on behind the scenes. Usually they know more than they seem to.

22½-25° Pisces
The tenth duad of Pisces is the Pisces-Sagittarius or Jupiter-Neptune-Jupiter duad. Because Jupiter rules both Pisces and Sagittarius, it has a double influence in this duad. These natives often have a keen imagination, strong religious leanings, and penetrating spiritual, intuitive, and prophetic insights. The influence of the Scorpio decanate combined with prophetic ability enables these natives to understand the underlying forces that will shape future cultural events and developments. These natives have an interest in the occult lore or mysticism of other cultures. They may travel in connection with secret missions of some sort.

25-27½° Pisces
The eleventh duad of Pisces is the Pisces-Capricorn or Jupiter-Neptune-Saturn duad. Inherent in this duad is a double-Mars influence that combines with the cardinal-earth influence of the Capricorn decanate to make these natives more practical and decisive than the average Pisces. Those with this duad prominent in the horoscope can be associated with secret police or intelligence activities such as the secret affairs of large corporations and government agencies. They may work in an administrative capacity in a hospital or institution, and are very resourceful in drawing on past experience and intuitive knowledge to solve professional and business problems. These natives are reserved, dignified, and quite capable of being forceful, but they reserve force until it will serve a useful purpose. Since Pisces is a mutable sign, Scorpio a fixed sign, and Capricorn is cardinal, there is a good blend of adaptability, determination, and decisiveness.

27½-30° Pisces
The twelfth duad of Pisces is the Pisces-Aquarius or Jupiter-Neptune-Uranus-Saturn duad. There is a double-Uranus influence inherent in this duad because of the Uranus rulership of the Aquarius duad and exaltation in Scorpio. If one of the outer planets is found here, those with this duad prominent will have exceptional psychic abilities. They are often involved in occult work or associated with secret aspects of scientific research or with secret organizations or groups. The Scorpio decanate and Aquarius duad combine to give great willpower and determination to overcome obstacles and to prepare for a new phase of experience. Because Aquarius is an air sign, these natives are more emotionally detached than the average Pisces.

www.ingramcontent.com/pod-product-compliance
Lightning Source LLC
Chambersburg PA
CBHW081840170426
43199CB00017B/2800